$1.50 $5.00
7 7

D0045794

Married to Me

© TANYA TRIBBLE STUDIO

 Married to Me

How Committing to Myself Led to Triumph After Divorce

DAYANARA TORRES
Former Miss Universe

WITH Jeannette Torres-Alvarez
Mental Health Counselor

A CELEBRA BOOK

CELEBRA

Published by New American Library, a division of Penguin Group (USA) Inc., 375 Hudson Street, New York, New York 10014, USA
Penguin Group (Canada), 90 Eglinton Avenue East, Suite 700, Toronto, Ontario M4P 2Y3, Canada (a division of Pearson Penguin Canada Inc.)
Penguin Books Ltd., 80 Strand, London WC2R 0RL, England
Penguin Ireland, 25 St. Stephen's Green, Dublin 2, Ireland (a division of Penguin Books Ltd.)
Penguin Group (Australia), 250 Camberwell Road, Camberwell, Victoria 3124, Australia (a division of Pearson Australia Group Pty. Ltd.)
Penguin Books India Pvt. Ltd., 11 Community Centre, Panchsheel Park, New Delhi - 110 017, India
Penguin Group (NZ), 67 Apollo Drive, Rosedale, North Shore 0632, New Zealand (a division of Pearson New Zealand Ltd.)
Penguin Books (South Africa) (Pty.) Ltd., 24 Sturdee Avenue, Rosebank, Johannesburg 2196, South Africa

Penguin Books Ltd., Registered Offices:
80 Strand, London WC2R 0RL, England

First published by Celebra,
a division of Penguin Group (USA) Inc.

First Printing, June 2008
10 9 8 7 6 5 4 3 2 1

Copyright © Dayanara Torres and Jeannette Torres-Alvarez, 2008
All rights reserved

CELEBRA and logo are trademarks of Penguin Group (USA) Inc.

LIBRARY OF CONGRESS CATALOGING-IN-PUBLICATION DATA:
Torres, Dayanara.
    Married to me: how committing to myself led to triumph after divorce/Dayanara Torres, with Jeannette Torres-Alvarez.
        p. cm.
    ISBN 978-0-451-22461-3
    1. Torres, Dayanara.   2. Divorced   women—Biography.   3. Divorced   women—Psychology.   4. Self-esteem in women.   I. Torres-Alvarez, Jeannette.   II. Title.
    HQ811.5.T67A3 2008
        306.89'3092—dc22   2008000794
[B]

Set in Joanna
Designed by Susan Hood

Printed in the United States of America

Without limiting the rights under copyright reserved above, no part of this publication may be reproduced, stored in or introduced into a retrieval system, or transmitted, in any form, or by any means (electronic, mechanical, photocopying, recording, or otherwise), without the prior written permission of both the copyright owner and the above publisher of this book.

PUBLISHER'S NOTE
The publisher does not have any control over and does not assume any responsibility for author or third-party Web sites or their content.
    The recipes contained in this book are to be followed exactly as written. The publisher is not responsible for your specific health or allergy needs that may require medical supervision. The publisher is not responsible for any adverse reactions to the recipes contained in this book.

The scanning, uploading, and distribution of this book via the Internet or via any other means without the permission of the publisher is illegal and punishable by law. Please purchase only authorized electronic editions, and do not participate in or encourage electronic piracy of copyrighted materials. Your support of the author's rights is appreciated.

To my chocolatitos, Cristian and Ryan,

Because my life has meaning since
you two chose me

CONTENTS

Married to Me

OPENING LETTER
FROM DAYANARA

I remember thinking, over and over again, what a shame it was that I wasted that dress. I know it was a silly thing to mourn, but it was so much easier than mourning the heavy things, my marriage, for instance. But it *was* a great dress. It was exactly the kind of dress I used to describe to my sister, Jeannette Torres-Alvarez, whom I refer to as Jinny, all of those afternoons after school when we spent countless teenage hours discussing weddings, boys, and bridesmaids. Of course, we never discussed breakups, divorces, or what to wear to a settlement hearing, but Lord knows we have spent countless adult hours discussing these very topics.

Jinny is a mental-health counselor with several degrees and years of practice under her belt, and don't think I didn't take advantage of all of this. Throughout my divorce, she was my stability, my best friend, and my on-hand therapist. Luckily for me, she wasn't charging—my Lord, that would have been a huge bill.

Jinny is the one with all of the experience, and she has read all of the books. Me, I never made it past the first few pages. I tried, I promise you. I went to every bookstore in the neighborhood and sought out that small, sad "divorce section." Even though the last thing I wanted was to read a book about divorce, I stood there, leafing through each cold, boring, depressing book. I bought a few anyway, to show that I was making an effort, I guess. I added them to my bookshelf and then never opened them again.

All I wanted was a book that was warm, conversational, even a little funny. Something that would help lighten all the pain I was feeling. The last thing I wanted to do was open up a textbook on divorce. I needed a sort of "girlfriends' guide to divorce," that would give me mantras, anecdotes, and some personal insight as to what I would be going through . . . but it didn't exist. So I decided to write it. I pulled Jinny into the fray (as usual). She is the one with the degrees, and I am the one with the divorce papers—together we make a good writing team. Throughout this book, I will present you with personal situations and advice, and Jinny will give you the professional lowdown. I have also peppered the text with my favorite quotes, which I collected in a notebook throughout my divorce. We hope that through our advice, anecdotes, stories, and quotes, we can both guide and inspire you. This is not a book about encouraging divorce. It is a book about encouraging your relationship with yourself (whether that self is divorced or not). This is the book I would have loved to find between the self-help and the sociology sections! It would have been a lot more helpful and constructive than all of the countless Lifetime movies I sulked through. Ultimately, I should be grateful I didn't find that perfect book because that is what inspired me to write my own. God knows, this book was not easy for me to write. It has taken years of sorrow and triumph for me to share with you and hopefully inspire you to take control of your life, commit to yourself, and become your truest, happiest self.

Always,
Dayanara ("Yari")

A NOTE FROM JINNY

alance ... Isn't that what all women want to achieve? I have felt the frustrations of not being able to find my balance, and I know that every woman I know has had similar frustrations. Achieving balance and living in harmony with our family, friends, partner, and those around us are not easy tasks. Writing this book has given me the opportunity to explore and discover what balance is all about.

There is a point in our lives when we start to juggle those glass balls—the aspects in our life that we hold valuable and do not want to let fall to the floor. We often find it hard to keep them all up in the air at the same time. For many of us, we are constantly juggling:

Motherhood—We are trying to be perfect mothers! We play with the smelly Pla-Doh. We come up with silly songs and dances so the children will eat their dinners. We make sure they don't eat too

much sugar so they will fall asleep easily and give us a few minutes to relax while we take a shower. And still, at the end of day, we
often wonder, "Am I doing a good job?"

Relationship—We are constantly trying to keep the flame alive. But
after eight hours of work, two hours of traffic (at least for some of
us), three hours of doing homework with the kids, cooking dinner (at least some of us), and trying to keep the house in order,
sometimes we don't have the energy. When we finally sit down for
a few moments, or at the end of the day, we often want to say, "I
just want to be left alone."

Work—We are constantly trying to keep our careers moving forward. We get up early, stay up late, and skip lunch, but it seems
that no matter what, the piles of paper and laundry never dwindle.
And at the end of the day, we often want to say, "Am I doing
enough?"

In Yari's case, these are definitely three of the balls that she is
constantly keeping up in the air, but for a while, it is true, she let
her career fall by the wayside. When she was first married, it was
beautiful and refreshing to see my sister so in love; it was definitely a type of love we don't see every day. As her sister, I sup-
ported the fact that she dedicated herself so completely to her
relationship and family; however, I was also concerned that she
decided not to pursue her career at the same time. I knew it was a
passion of hers and it was very valuable to her happiness. At first,
it did not seem to affect her all that much. She seemed happy to
focus on motherhood and her marriage. However, after a while,
she came to realize that her life was not in total harmony and balance. She had let that third glass ball drop.

Today, I am so happy to see with my own eyes how my sister,
my best friend, has achieved her balance again. I am extremely
proud to see that Yari is an amazing mother, giving Cristian and

baby Ryan no less than the best of herself. She is a successful and inspirational *professional*, once again committed to her work and her passion. And she has once again been able to enter into a happy and healthy *relationship*, because she has taken the time to establish a happy and healthy relationship with *herself*. The fact that my sister has found the balance she was looking for for so long means the world to me!

While I was spending hours on this project, my husband asked me about the audience for this book. I deeply believe this book is directly targeted to all women. Whether you are single, married, divorced, or separated, this book is aimed at you. You may be juggling different priorities, but the message is the same for each and every one of you: BALANCE.

I wish all of you, by reading this book, can move toward finding your own **BALANCE** in life.

Best,
Jinny

INTRODUCTION

I*n case you want* to get your money back before you break the binding, I want to tell you this is not a tell-all book. Far from it. First of all, we work very hard to maintain a healthy family identity. Second, I could never make my divorce as interesting or dramatic as the tabloids made it out to be. Honestly, it wasn't actually that ugly. We didn't fight over a single kitchen appliance. *That's* how dramatic our divorce proceedings were.

That's not to say my divorce was an easy experience. My God, no. I just didn't care enough about the blender to spend my days fighting over it. I had other things to do, and to worry about, like my kids and my future. In the meantime, however, I spent a good deal of time crying, I watched hours of Lifetime movies, and I ate more than my fair share of comfort food. You need to do whatever it takes to get your head out of the stress, pain, and anxiety. I highly recommend losing a few hours—hell, even a whole day—to

Lifetime movies. I promise you, your life will seem less pathetic in comparison. The comfort foods? Any comfort food is most definitely allowed. It's all allowed. Whatever works, whatever makes you feel any better about this mess is *allowed*.

Oh, and let's be honest. It's a mess. There is a reason Jinny and I didn't sit on our beds as teenagers and dreamily proclaim, "When I get divorced, I'm going to wear a beautifully cut black Armani suit, and my 'divorce maids' are going to wear bloodred." No, it is never supposed to end in divorce, so it's hard to recover from the blow that your love story is not going to end in happily ever after.

My love story began in 1999, when I met my ex-husband in Puerto Rico. I had been crowned Miss Universe six years earlier, and after that day, I had not stopped working, traveling, and moving around (from Puerto Rico, to LA, to the Philippines, and back to Puerto Rico). I was tired, hungry for some stability, and ready to be swept off my feet. My ex-husband came along at just the right moment. We seemed to share all the same values and dreams. He wanted to settle down, start a family, and share his successes with someone. I felt exactly the same way. We started dating, and it was only a matter of months before we were engaged. I could not have been happier.

We were married on May 10, 2000, in a civil ceremony in Las Vegas. Two years later we renewed our vows in a grand fashion in San Juan, where I finally got my dream wedding. After four years we decided that we no longer shared the same values and dreams. We finalized our divorce in June 2004, and my fairy tale came to a screeching halt. I could not have been more devastated. Purely and utterly devastated. You see, I'm a fairy tale kind of girl. I've wanted the happily-ever-after since before I can remember. I had already envisioned our entire life together: the anniversaries, the vacations, the birthdays, the children, and most of all the weekends.

When I was a child, Jinny, my brothers, and I would pile into my parents' bed on Saturday and Sunday mornings. We would stay there for hours, talking, joking, and laughing. As I grew older, I held on to the image of those mornings, and I always thought that I would share these same kind of moments with my family. I wanted my children to have the feeling of love and security and joy that I felt during those times. And I wanted them to have the same kinds of holidays I remembered too, with both of their parents there to photograph the opening of the gifts and the cutting of the birthday cake. I wanted them to have both of their parents standing on the Little League sidelines during every game. I wanted the holiday cards to show a perfect family unit every year. The problem, I realize now, is that these memories were all rooted in happiness. In order to give my sons these memories, I had to be honest with myself and admit that I was not longer happy in my marriage.

I wanted the sitting-in-our-rocking-chairs-with-gray-hair ending so badly. I did not want the I'll-take-this-house-and-you'll-take-that-house ending. And yet, in December 2003, I found myself in a law office in Miami, signing an I'll-take-this-house-you'll-take-that-house document. When I walked out of that office, I had no idea what to do with myself. I stood in that obnoxiously bright Miami sun and said, "Okay, now what." Then a part of me answered, "Hell if I know." Another part of me suggested, "Let's go home and lie in bed and cry for a little while." So, because I couldn't come up with a better option, that is just what I did.

Lying in that bed, I had days when I thought I would never recover from the divorce. Of course, there were friends and family members who would tell me, "You're going to be fine! This is going to make you stronger!" Oh, how I wanted to slug them. I just wanted to reel back and really slug them. If only I had had the strength. Instead, I just crawled deeper under the covers, put the pillow over my face, and wailed, "This isn't how it was supposed to happen!" Dramatic? Perhaps. Deserved? Definitely. For at least the first few weeks (oh, maybe months), I deserved to wail into that pillow. I'm sure there were friends and family members who wanted to shake me and repeat those annoying assurances: "You're going to be fine! This is going to make you stronger!" But they didn't. They were smarter than that. They saw from the look in my puffy eyes that I didn't need any of their peppy mantras. At that point, the only mantras I wanted to hear were along the lines of: "You've lost weight!" and "Your hair actually looks good when you don't wash it!"

It is only now, as I sit down to write this book, that I realize I barely recognize the girl who was wailing into the pillow four years ago. And it is only now that I can finally admit that maybe all of those friends and family members with their peppy you're-going-to-be-fine mantras were right. Yes, okay, they were right. Today, I am so much better than fine. Today, after a four-year trek from that depressing Miami law office to my happy new Los Angeles home, I can say that I am stronger than I ever thought possible.

Yes, it took me four full years to get to this healthy, happy, hair-washing-on-a-regular-basis place. I did not rush myself. I took my time and enjoyed every step of the journey. A few months after the divorce, for no logical reason, I decided to cut my hair and dye it red. Red? (I thought it looked okay until I was in the Miami airport and someone said to me, "Oh, you don't look that bad with the red hair. I don't know what everyone is talking about." Oof. If you want to know the truth about anything, head to the Miami airport.) I dyed my hair back to black shortly after that, and that was when I started happily dating . . . my three-year-old-son. I took Cristian out for regular dinner-and-a-movie Saturday nights (my sons make great dates), and I started to feel like myself again. Then, one full year after the divorce—when every holiday did not remind me of last year's holiday with my ex—I began to establish my own traditions with the boys. After that first year, once I was confident enough, I started taking steps at a somewhat quicker pace. I went back to work, made plans to move to LA, took myself on trips, etc. But still, I refused to rush myself in my recovery. I'm not ashamed to say that it took me four years to recover fully.

It took me four years before I could sit down and write this book as I wanted to write it—from an honest, healthy, happy place. My hope is that, by telling you my story as candidly as possible (puffy eyes and red hair dye included), I will help inspire you in your journey to happiness and rediscovery. Today, after a long journey of rediscovery, I am proud to say that I am committed to myself before anyone else. Yes, it took me four years, but I have finally traded in my engagement ring for a diamond-encrusted Cartier watch. It was way too expensive and all too well worth it. I see it as my engagement ring to myself, because today I finally realize that the first person you have to marry in life is yourself.

Now, on weekend mornings, the boys pile into my bed, and we talk and joke and laugh. Sometimes I wonder if we would have these kinds of weekend mornings if I had stayed in my marriage. I truly don't think we would, because I would not have been the happy, healthy, strong mother that I am. Today, I am the kind of mother who can juggle the video camera and the birthday cake quite adeptly. I am the kind of mother who proudly sends out perfect holiday cards every December, who chases after her dreams every morning, and who manages to pick up the boys from school every afternoon. The other night, as I was putting the boys to bed, my older boy began his prayers by saying, "Thank you, God, for all of the memories that my mom gives me." At times like these, I realize that I have not taken anything away from these boys at all. Instead, I have given them the kind of mother they deserve.

Part One

Acceptance

*Realizing the Reality
of the Situation*

"You drown not by falling in a river,
but by staying submerged in it."
—*Paulo Coelho*

I was in our new house in Miami when we made the decision. We had been there a week. None of the walls were painted, and I had just ordered all of our furniture, so I was sleeping on a mattress on the floor. I guess I could have gone back to Long Island and stayed in the much nicer house—the house that was fully decorated, fully stocked, had much more square footage, and a real bed for me to throw myself onto in dramatic grief. But I did not want to return to that place; I knew it would be too painful to attempt my recovery in a home where we had lived together for four years. All of the good and the not-so-good memories memories would have haunted me on a daily basis. The Miami house had no such memories. It was devoid of any old ghosts, which made the environment comfortable, tension-free, and all mine. But the best part about Miami, and the biggest reason that I stayed, was because Jinny and Mom lived there, and I knew that I could never move forward without them by my side.

For the first few months in Miami, I do not think I moved forward at all. How is it possible to move forward when all you want to do is lie in bed? Honestly, that is what I did for months. There were days when I never untangled myself from the sheets. My remote control was my best friend. By my bedside, I had a few of those horrible divorce books, which I thought about reading, but never did. Who feels like reading twenty chapters (in small print, no less) about freaking divorce? That's where Jinny came in; she told me if I had read the books I would have known the stages and phases I would have to go through to get myself up out of that bed. I looked at Jinny and said, "Why read the books when you can just tell me?" So she rattled them off, and in that one breath, I realized that I was not alone. I recognized that my experience, although unique and unfathomable to me, was universal. There are generations of strong women who have endured the pain of divorce and the resilience of rebuilding. This was so apparent because the five phases made so much sense.

> I. Denial
> II. Anger
> III. Guilt
> IV. Pain
> V. Acceptance

The first four didn't sound so fun. The last one didn't sound possible. But, little by little, just as Jinny said, I began moving through the stages without even realizing I was doing so. I was right about Denial, Anger, Guilt, and Pain. They aren't so fun. But I was wrong about the Acceptance stage. It is possible, it will come, but it is up to you to get yourself there.

Though I didn't think I needed the books or any of the professional terminology to help me get through the great recovery, it helped me enormously to hear Jinny speak those words: Denial, Anger, Guilt, and Pain. It meant that all of my emotions were natural and normal. After struggling through so many grief-ridden days, I couldn't help but wonder, Is this okay? I am telling you, it took all the strength I had to get up and brush my teeth. I felt a little pathetic, and I kept thinking, Is this what everyone goes through? Is this normal? So when Jinny spoke those four words, I thought, Okay, so at least I am not being more pathetic and dramatic than every other divorcée in the world. At least other women out there had trouble putting the Crest on the bristles. So yes, I guess the professional terminology is helpful, to a certain degree, but I truly didn't need any long-winded technical explications. What I needed was a short personal explanation of each stage followed by a short professional explanation. This is exactly what you can expect to find in the following pages. We will be short, sweet, honest, and to the point. We know that you have things to do, Lifetime movies to watch. This first section on Acceptance will lead you through each of the stages from both a personal and professional standpoint. I am going to let you in on my personal journey, the obstacles I faced, and how I finally arrived at the Acceptance stage. Throughout this segment, you will also find the notes and advice that Jinny gave me along the way. Though I know that our journeys are not the same, I am sure that we faced many of the same stumbling blocks in some form or another. In fact, every divorcée I know has faced most, if not all of the hurdles I have. We stumbled over them at different rates and with varying degrees of beginner's luck. Each time I discovered that I was not the only person in the world who wondered if I was at fault for the entire divorce, and I was not the only person who let myself wallow in my pain for days at a time. I found that just knowing that the hurdles are there for everyone gave me a great deal of comfort and support. In the interest of offering you some comfort and support, I'll share each hurdle that I had to leap (and sometimes stumble) over to get myself to the place where I could finally accept the reality of the situation, which to be honest, is one of the most difficult parts of the process.

The First of Many Short Professional Explanations from Jinny

Note from Jinny

ON THE FIVE STAGES

It is important to recognize that you will move through all of these stages, but in your own manner and at your own pace. These five stages should serve as basic guidelines for the emotional phases of a breakup. This is not a checklist. You will not necessarily go through one and then move on to the next. For example, you may feel the Guilt while you are in the Pain stage, or vice versa. Do not think that you are "doing it wrong" if you don't move swiftly and cleanly from one to the next. It is very rare that women actually glide right through in an orderly fashion. It is also important to remember that each person moves through these emotional stages at his or her own pace. Do not worry that you are "not moving fast enough." Give yourself time. Some women spend years in the Denial stage, while others spend mere hours. It depends on how invested (emotionally, physically, and financially) one was in the relationship.

No marriage is the same; therefore, no divorce will be the same, and there is no format for how each person recovers.

I also want to take the time to note here that not every bad marriage has to end in divorce. If you are contemplating divorce, or you are in a relationship that you are not presently satisfied with, this book can be an incredibly useful tool for you. It can help you recognize what needs to be mended in your relation-ship and hopefully guide you in way to help you and your partner heal. If, after trying hard to work on your relationship, the not-so-good times outnumber the good times, then perhaps it is time to contemplate divorce.

THE STAGES OF ACCEPTANCE
Denial, Anger, Guilt, Pain . . . and Acceptance

STAGE I: *Denial*

"Denial ain't just a river in Egypt."—Mark Twain

The first thing that happens when your marriage falls apart is that you enter into a state of denial. And I have to say, I was pretty good at this stage (or horrible, depending on how you look at it). I ac-tually went through this stage during my marriage and stayed here for quite a long time, telling myself that things weren't so bad, that everything would get better, and that we just had to ride out the storm. I truly believed this, because when we had good days, they would be amazing days. On those days I would think, "Okay, we are fine. We are like every other couple in the world with good days and bad days." I would not allow myself to admit that the good days came so few and far between. I just could not admit the truth because I so badly wanted to believe that we were not headed for divorce. It was just not part of my plan, and I am one of those people who make a plan and stick to it. In the interest of my sticking with the "perfectly planned life" I had set up, I completely denied how I was feeling. I refused to admit how badly I was hurting, that I felt nauseous most days and that I felt like I was going to collapse. No, not me. I was fine. I was better than fine. I had found the person I wanted to spend the rest of my life with and that was it—we were going to grow old together, *dammit*. I allowed myself to swim around in this denial for several reasons:

Reason #1) I was always taught to "stick it out." Where I grew up, nobody got divorced. Most people I knew "stuck out" bad marriages, abusive relationships, and cheating spouses. "Till death do you part" was taken to heart, and who was I to challenge those words? Nope, I was going to stick it out too, for better or for worse.

Reason #2) I hate failure. I was always the girl who had perfect grades and perfect attendance in school. I have the trophies to prove it! I remember distinctly the one day I missed. It was the day they taught us the Pythagorean theorem. I failed the test, and it still haunts me. And that was algebra for goodness' sake—this was a marriage. And, dammit, I wasn't going to fail.

Reason #3) We had kids together. I was raised in a two-parent household, and I desperately wanted to give my children the same, stable environment. I did not want to deny my children the nuclear family. I did not want to fail my children.

I thought these reasons were sound, strong, and to a certain extent, I still do. But there came a time when I subconsciously began to refute each of these reasons. Who cares what everyone else has done? So what if I said "for better or for worse"? Won't I be a better parent if I'm a happier parent? These pseudo-mantras were all chanted during bouts of confidence and self-assurance. I say "pseudo-mantra" because I think I only half believed in them. I have to admit that my bouts of doubt and self-consciousness came much more often, and I would retreat into my "sound, strong" reasons. I was comfortable with them. I wanted to believe in them; if I did, nothing had to change, and I didn't have to take responsibility. Did you notice how each "pseudo-mantra" came in the form of a question? I was very unsure of myself, and I was looking for somebody to give me an answer. And yet I was asking these questions of myself, waiting for the day that I would be strong enough to stand up and take responsibility for my own situation.

And then the day came when I realized that I was a shell of the person I had once been. This is something that my friends and family had gently tried to tell me for months, but I had to be the one to realize it. I had to admit fully that I was no longer the woman I had been when my ex-husband and I met. Was that my fault? His fault? At that point, I did not care about placing blame. I just knew that I didn't want to waste another day living as a woman who I barely knew.

Who had I been before? I was a fun-loving, funny, vivacious person. I had interests and hobbies. I was the girl who threw the biggest parties, who danced the longest, who sang the loudest. And all of a sudden, I was the girl who never threw parties, who never danced, who never sang. All of a sudden, my sense of adventure was gone. I was too overwhelmed to drive into Manhattan alone. In fact I didn't drive at all. All of a sudden, I found myself spending entire days not leaving the house, just waiting for nighttime so I could go to sleep. But in reality, it wasn't all of a sudden; it was a gradual process that I hardly acknowledged. This is why it took me so long to finally wake up and see what I had done to my former self. I had been in a trance of denial for so long that I did not realize that by keeping myself in a not so happy situation, I had slowly been killing off my spunk and spirit—the part of me I have always loved most of all. I had one great friend who would tell me, "You are not yourself. You've lost your sparkle. You can change this, Yari." I did not want to hear it then, but I remember looking in the mirror one day and seeing a profound sadness in my eyes, which had once sparkled with that spirit. And that was when I heard my own faraway voice tell me, "You are not yourself. You've lost your sparkle. You can change this, Yari." That day, that moment, I decided I was going to listen to that inner voice, which I finally let speak to me. And that was when I moved on to the next stage. . . .

Note from Jinny

ON DENIAL

Denial is a nice, comfortable place. You can tell yourself that there is hope that things will get better. You can tell yourself that you do not need to leave, nothing has to change, and everything will be fine if you just ride out the storm. The reality is, you are protecting yourself from the truth, and you are protecting your loved ones, or at least you think you are protecting them. You are creating an armor that shields you from the truth.

It is a heavy armor to carry, and one day, you are going to have to take it off. This will be liberating. You are letting yourself see the reality of your situation, and you can finally breathe. But it can also be frightening when you realize that without the armor, you are leaving yourself open to judgment, pain, and change. This is okay. You will be okay. That armor wasn't protecting you from anything that you cannot handle yourself. You are stronger than the armor of denial.

STAGE II: *Anger*

"Holding on to anger is like grasping a hot coal with the intent of throwing it at someone else; you are the one who gets burned."—Buddha

The Anger stage reared its ugly head once I dropped the denial and accepted the reality of the situation. For me, I felt as though I was standing alone, armorless, awaiting a world of pain and judgment. And so what was the natural thing to do? Look for somebody to blame, of course! And who better to blame than the person who put me in this situation: my ex-husband. *Everything* became his fault. He did this and he did that. I blamed him for all my pain and suffering. I was furious.

Now I realize that you simply have to be angry. Be angry at the broken dream, the broken promises, the broken life, but if you have children, try not to do this in front of them. I can see how easy it is to fall into this trap. I have seen this happen all too often, and it is terrible to watch. I have friends who still carry baggage from hearing their mothers bashing their fathers on a regular basis. With this knowledge, I knew to never, ever vent my anger in front of my children. I did not want my children to choose sides or feel like they had any part in this mess. That's what you have sisters and friends for. This is the stage when I phoned my sister and my best friends and vented—and because my sister and friends are smart, they just sat on the other ends of the lines and listened. And that is exactly what I needed. I didn't need anyone to join me in my anger. If my family and friends did harbor anger for my ex-husband, I didn't need to hear about it. I still don't. It was my marriage, my divorce, so I needed to work through my anger, not anybody else's.

In the anger stage, you will probably paint your ex-husband as the devil and yourself as the angel in every scenario. And while I am sure you are quite a lovely person, I am also sure that you had a little something to do with the situation. I know I did. But you don't need anyone telling you that now! This will all come later. What you need now is a group of friends who will just listen.

Not all of your friends and family may be willing to do this. That is fine and completely normal. I did have friends whom I had to stay away from for a little while, no matter how much I loved them. There are always going to be friends who do not know how to just listen, but want to offer you advice or start talking trash. For your own sake, you have to hold these friends at arm's length for a little while and stick close to the friends and family who can and will just listen. I was so lucky to have friends and family who knew how to do just that, and their doing so was the very best gift that they could have given me, because I think that it made my anger stage short. How fun is it to be the only one calling names? How fun is it to be angry all the time? So what is left to do but pick up your things and move on down the road.

Note from Jinny

ON ANGER

Once you realize the reality of the situation, anger begins to set in, and it is true, everything will become your ex-husband's fault. You will blame him for all of the big things and all of the little things. This is because you are not yet ready to take your own part of the responsibility for the breakup. You will feel as though you are incompetent and a failure, and you need someone besides yourself to blame for this. Go ahead, blame him for a little while. A period of anger is necessary and beneficial. It can help you stop being dependent and feeling like a victim. But while it is necessary and helpful to feel this anger, it is also hurtful to hold on to it too long. It can become self-defeating, self-destructive, and the root of bad judgment. When you act out of anger, you are not acting on a rational level. And the result is not only that you feel miserable, but you find yourself acting in a way you never have before.

Anger is cheap and easy, easier than actually solving your real problems, and easier than taking responsibility for your life; however, it only distracts you from having to face your pain, fear, or guilt. If you get stuck in this angry place, it will poison your life and turn you into an unhealthy, lonely, bitter person.

You will drop the anger and blame in your own time, though it won't be easy. It can take a long time, but every day you hold on to this anger, you are losing a day in your recovery process. In order to fully recover, you have to begin to feed your own soul, and breaking down another person will not help to do this. In fact, it has the opposite effect. Harboring anger slowly eats away at you, and you have that much farther to go in your journey to full rediscovery.

STAGE III: *Guilt*

"Guilt—the gift that keeps on giving."—Erma Bombeck

I moved through anger pretty quickly. Guilt I did not. I sputtered here, and actually, I still struggle with it. There are so many things to feel guilty about, and I think it is very natural, at some point, to start blaming yourself for everything that went wrong and worrying about the implications of your decision to divorce. I know I did. All of my thoughts were mixed, and I started to doubt myself. I was my own worst enemy during this stage, as I lay awake, bogging myself down with guilty questions, such as:

1. Was it all my fault? After the anger stage, where I declared that everything was his fault, I fell into the trap of thinking that maybe everything was my fault. I call this the "shoulda, coulda, woulda" question. I should have been stronger. I could have stayed a little longer. I would have stuck up for myself a little more. I'd get trapped in this fruitless thinking for hours at a time, but the truth is all of the "shoulda, coulda, woulda" in the world will not change the reality of the situation you are in now. So the best thing for me to do was stop the guilty cycle and move on, which is easier said than done, because I found so many more things to be guilty about, including:

2. How could I do this to my children? How could I take away their perfect family unit? It was hard for me to justify divorcing my husband, when I had seen my mother stick out a not so happy marriage for thirty years and all "for the sake of the kids." She made the sacrifice for us, and I wanted to make that sacrifice for my children too. But it took me a while to see that in "making that sacrifice," I would also be sacrificing the type of mother I wanted to be. I wanted to be a happy, fun mother who was 100 percent there for my children. I realized that maybe it would have been better for everyone involved if my husband and I separated, and instead of being angry and unhappy parents living in the same house, we could be peaceful and happy parents who lived a few miles apart. But there was a lot of guilt involved before I could see that I was not taking away my children's "perfect family unit," because it simply isn't a perfect family unit if both of the parents are miserable. Yet I still feel guilt some days and feel that I "took away their father," which brings me to my third major guilt:

3. How could I take away my sons' father figure? Because I had two boys, I felt extreme guilt in knowing that I was taking away their male role model. I still struggle with this guilt, and I am constantly striving to serve as both a mother and a father figure in their everyday lives. My guilt was so strong that I did all sorts of crazy things to try to make myself less fearful and more "fatherly." I trained myself not to "scream like a girl" when I saw a lizard (my biggest fear). I stopped watching scary movies altogether so I would not get scared of noises in the night. I taught myself all of the *Star Wars* characters and learned how to play video games (I'm still really bad, though). It was just me and them now, and I knew that I had to fulfill the roles that my husband would have normally taken on, so I am still overconscious of being fatherly and motherly at the same time. I have realized that I am one of the only mothers at the Little League field who intently focuses on the game and not my BlackBerry. I am the one intensely yelling, "Hey, stop playing with the grass! Pay attention! Eye on the ball!" (Though I feel that this may have less to do with the fact that I am divorced and more to do with the fact that I am from Puerto Rico, and we do not play with the grass during baseball games.)

How long does this guilt last? I'd like to tell you I know how long it lasts because I've overcome it, but I have to be honest—to this day, I feel guilty. It comes and goes. I could be having a great day, feeling as though I am on top of the world, and then there will be an activity at school that just sends me into a tailspin. I see all the other kids who are so excited to see their moms and dads arriving, taking pictures and videos of the play. And then there's me. A mess. Two cameras, a big bag with my stuff, an extra CD and battery for the video camera, extra chips and AA batteries for the still camera. I can do only one at a time! I feel so guilty, because I feel like I took "normal" away from us. But I have to tell myself that normal is not the same anymore. I have to believe it. I remind myself that I did not separate my kids from their father, but I separated myself from my husband, and that was best for us all. I am not saying that divorce is the answer. We tried our best to make it work, and we just couldn't. Now I know that this is my life; me fumbling with two cameras is our "normal." After a few years of practice, I'm taking some pretty great pictures.

Note from Jinny

ON GUILT

It is perfectly natural to start blaming yourself for everything. You will start to believe that the entire divorce was your fault. *It was not.* I promise you, it is not possible for an entire divorce to be one person's fault. Just as two people are responsible for a healthy relationship, two people are responsible for an unhealthy relationship. That being said, it is not easy to see this in the middle of your divorce, and most likely you will spend an inordinate amount of time beating yourself up about every little thing that you "could have, should have, and would have" done differently.

This is often the stage where depression sets in. You are stuck in this cycle of self-blame, and you start to doubt your own character and your abilities in life. You need to remind yourself that you are fundamentally a good person. That you are fun, attractive, smart, kind. But more important, that you are lovable and have never ceased to be. Find somebody to talk to who will just listen. You may be lucky enough to have such a person in your life, but if not, seek out a therapist or a life coach. Just getting your feelings out there will help you to see that it was not all your fault or his fault. The fact of the matter is that your relationship to each other has changed, and you are now strong and smart enough to see that your marriage is no longer healthy.

STAGE IV: *Pain*

"For after all, the best thing one can do when it's raining is to let it rain."—Henry Wadsworth Longfellow

I never before understood the pain that a divorce brings. All of those dramatic breakups, those boyfriends gone, were nothing in comparison to this. This time I had built a life, had children, and had planned far into the future with this man. We had picked out furniture, established traditions, and fused our lives together so completely. It was meant to be forever, and that was how we had both truly and so deeply believed that it would be. But then our relationship began to crumble, and we made the decision to divorce, it was as if my whole world had come crashing down right on top of me. I was stuck under the rubble and couldn't even conceive of digging myself out. For a good, long while I just lay there, stupefied and saddened and profoundly crushed. What happens now? All of my dreams, that beautiful ending to my love story, the future plans—they all lay scattered around me. I was too pained to know where to start picking up the pieces. Part of me, a very selfish part, didn't want to even try.

I can honestly say I was a different person at this time. My priorities were out of whack, my life was upside down, and so I just sat there (or lay there, depending on the time of day) and wallowed in the pain. This may sound like an awful waste of time, but I don't think I would have been able to fully heal unless I let myself feel this pain. In my opinion it was a necessary—albeit very unglamorous—chapter in my recovery. I moped about, forgetting to eat (divorce is a great way to lose weight!), staying in my pajamas for days. My legs didn't see a razor for weeks. Some days, I would just stare up at the ceiling and think about my pain, and the more I thought about my pain, the deeper I would go into it. As odd as it may seem, every day that I retreated into this pain was so necessary for me, just as every day I spent in my anger was necessary. You can't skip these crappy steps in order to take the not so crappy steps. Just put one foot in front of the other and know that one day some of this is going to be funny. Not all of it, and not for a little while, but I promise you, you will laugh at yourself! The other day, I took out my old notebook and started laughing at how dramatic I was in my writing. The basic refrain was "How am I going to go on?!" At the time I know I was miserable, but today, being so happy, I barely recognize the woman who wrote the words in that notebook.

Note from Jinny

ON PAIN

The pain may sound like the worst part of all of this, but it is actually the most helpful. Don't try to reject or run from the pain. You need to go through it in order to heal. If you reject your pain at the onset of the divorce, it will catch up with you later in full force. The truth of the matter is you have suffered a loss, and like any other loss, it must be mourned. You are saying goodbye to a big part of your life, and the pain, the crying, and the suffering are an acknowledgment of this.

Accept the pain, endure it, and listen to it. If you do, it will run its course and heal more quickly. It will lead you to your solutions. It will provide the energy for your changes and growth. And most important, it will make you *stronger.*

STAGE V: *Acceptance*

"Happiness can only exist in acceptance."
—Denis de Rougamont

Acceptance. The stage I never thought possible. Everyone kept telling me, "You'll get there. You'll get there." And I kept thinking, "Oh, be quiet. What do you know?"

But that's not a very good argument when everyone around you has either gone through a divorce, had friends or family go through a divorce, or been a divorce counselor. Perhaps they knew a little something? But at the beginning, I was not ready to see what they saw. So I just smiled politely and carried on, working through those other four stages, where I thought I would stay forever.

There is something safe and oddly comforting about bouncing between varying states of guilt, anger, denial, and pain. In each of these four stages you can play the victim and stay weak, and everyone can pity you. Your other option is to play the hero and stay strong, and everyone can admire you. I think I fell somewhere in the middle, floundering between victim and hero. What scares me is how easily I could have remained stuck in the victim mode. I've known women who have spent their lives playing the victim, never fully arriving at the acceptance stage; I think that these women have yet to arrive at true happiness. I have also known women who have not played the victim for one minute. They remained strong, and they chose to be their own heroes from day one. It seems to me that these women always end up happier than the victims. I learned something very valuable from both of these groups, the victims and the heroes, I had to make a decision. Did I want to be a happy hero, or did I want to be a miserable victim? Ah, how easy the decision looks on paper. Happy hero or miserable victim? You choose "happy hero" every time when you see it written down, yet in the reality of life, "miserable victim" can feel pretty decent some days. People pity the miserable victim. They dote on her and cook her favorite comfort food, and they don't judge her when she lies in bed all day and watches old Audrey Hepburn movies (at least I think they don't). But eventually, after months of denial, anger, guilt, pain, I was tired of being pitied, tired of being sad, and tired of being tired all the time. I had worn myself out, I was sick of Lifetime movies, and I had exhausted my collection of Audrey DVDs. When I realized that I could recite all the words to *Breakfast at Tiffany's*, *Funny Face*, *Roman Holiday*, *Charade*, and *My Fair Lady*, I thought, "Well, that is probably an indication that I have pitied myself enough." I got up out of bed, admitted to myself that this was really happening, told Audrey that we needed to take a break for a little while, and started looking forward.

"The most important thing is to enjoy life—to be happy—that's all that matters."—Audrey Hepburn

Note from Jinny

ON ACCEPTANCE

This is the step that will set you free, but it is the hardest to swallow. The Acceptance phase is not generally a time of great joy or celebration. It is simply a time when you fully come to terms with your divorce. You will finally let go of the hope that you can fix everything and that everything will work out.

You are ready to clear the air and move forward. This is the moment when you are ready to "change your filter," as I call it. The idea is that in life we create a filter to deal with the situations we are faced with. When you are healthy, the filter is clear, and when you are not, the filter is clogged, and it is hard for you to breathe. The day you decide to change your filter is the day you accept the reality of the situation. You are no longer the victim, and you can let go of your resentment and *be happy.* The air will begin to clear, and you will start to breathe easier.

The future is ahead of you. The good and the not so good times with your partner belong in the past. While there will always be a place in your heart for the relationship, it no longer defines your life—you no longer yearn for the past. Your future is what matters now.

*"La esperanza es lo último que se pierde.
(Hope is the last thing that we lose.)"*
—Spanish Proverb

The Tools

*Helping Yourself
Move Through the Stages
of Acceptance*

"God's greatest act was to
make one day follow another."
—*Puerto Rican Proverb*

The sun will obnoxiously continue to rise every single morning, for it has no mercy on the miserable. I remember it waking me up with all of its annoying warmth, imploring me to make something of the day, to get myself closer to that big goal of complete Acceptance. But how? I wanted to know. The sun never answered, but just kept on rising and forced me to find my own answers. Day by day, I discovered that each of the stages that Jinny outlined were normal and necessary; I just had to let them happen and take the struggles one at a time. It sounds crazy, but I actually started to enjoy the process and the pain, because it meant that I was healing. Over time I began to reconnect my emotional self with my physical self and I established ten "tools" or "mantras" that helped me to move through the stages at my own pace, without getting stuck . . . and without cursing the sun every morning.

Here are my ten tools; feel free to steal from them, add to them, delete from them:

1. Take the High Road
2. Let Go of Regret
3. Cry
4. Laugh
5. Rely on Others
6. Trust Yourself
7. Respect Your Ex
8. Commit to Yourself
9. Believe That Life Is Fair
10. Embrace Life

These tools may seem simplistic and idealistic, but believe me, it took me quite a while to pin them down and even longer to employ all ten of them (okay, maybe I'm still working on one or two). I found that if I stuck to these mantras, I felt a lot better about myself come sunset.

1. Take the High Road

"You cannot build happiness off of another's suffering."—Puerto Rican Proverb

The high road is not the easiest road to take. There is a road farther below, where you are free to sling mud and nobody is going to stop you. Most of the time, they will join in. I decided early that I wanted no part of the mudslinging and the trash talk. In many ways, the decision was made for me. I could never talk badly about my children's father. Just because we have decided to part ways doesn't mean I have to hate him or lose the respect I have for him. Even when the kids are not around, when they are at school or at a friend's house, I won't do it. I refuse to let any negative talk about my ex-husband enter my home. I do not want my sons to have any negative perceptions of their father. My friends and family know and respect this. I have worked hard to create a safe, healthy environment for my children; in doing so, I have also created a safe, healthy environment for myself.

I can see how easy it is to fill your days talking badly about your ex. It can feel reassuring to hear a resounding chorus of friends and family say how awful he is and how great you are. But as tempting as it was, I never wanted to hear that. Okay, maybe I wanted to hear it once or twice at the beginning, but deep down I knew that it would never bring me closer to coming to terms with what happened. I knew that I would only be happy again when I was at peace with my ex-husband, but most important, when I was at peace with myself. How could I be at peace if I was constantly trying to bring another person down to build myself up? I have seen women waste hours, days, lives away speaking ill of their ex-husbands. I have always felt bad for these women, because despite what they think, I know they are stuck in an unhappy place and that no amount of gossip is going to get them out of that rut.

I have also seen women gracefully pick up the pieces, keep their heads up, and move on down the high road. These are the women I have always admired, and so I set out to follow in their tracks.

Note from Jinny

ON TAKING THE HIGH ROAD

This is not always easy, especially when your ex is not playing by the rules, or if others are talking badly about you. Be nice anyway. No matter how others may be acting toward you, you are going to feel so much better when you walk with the knowledge that you are acting as a classy, strong, mature player in the divorce. Walk this high road long enough, and everyone around you will start to walk with you.

2. *Let Go of Regret*

"Turn your face to the sun and the shadows fall behind you."—Maori Proverb

I am lucky, because I come from a family where we do not look back—we only look forward. That is the blessing of coming from humble beginnings; you understand the uselessness of the words "what if." Instead, you learn how to say, "Okay, this is life. Let's move forward." When I was younger, I remember that at one point my family had to declare bankruptcy. But as dramatic and final as that sounds, surprisingly enough, I do not remember it as such a devastating event. It was just the reality of the situation. Nobody fretted or worried. We all took that "Okay, this is life. Let's move forward" attitude. That isn't to say that we didn't realize the gravity of the situation, but after that happened, I understood just how strong we were and how nothing could break us as a family. It made me feel so safe and secure. So, with each decision I made and each step I took in my divorce, I tried to keep those seven words in mind.

I am not going to say that I did not have days when I looked back in regret, spiraling hopelessly downward into the land of "what if" and "if only." I definitely had those days, no matter how hard I tried to suppress those useless words. It is only natural to have regrets. I shouldn't have been so eager to please. I shouldn't have given up my dreams. I shouldn't have put my career on hold. You can go over the whole register of your marriage and think about all that you should have done differently. You can continually wish that you had taken back certain statements, actions, arguments, even entire days. But we all know that that's not the way life works. You cannot undo the past, but you can learn from it. I learned to turn all of my "regrets" into "resolutions."

My biggest regret was that I did not speak up for myself more during my marriage. I let others make decisions for me—not just my husband, but my friends and family members too—from where we were going to dinner to what we were watching on TV to where we would spend Christmas. I just played follow the leader. The fact of the matter is that I did let others make my decisions. I could not change that. I could, however, resolve to myself that I will not let this happen again. Where once I regretted being too emotionally timid, I have now resolved to make myself strong and outspoken because I've realized that repressing my thoughts or wishes only resulted in pent-up frustration and even sadness. And that's not the person I want to be. I have to say that nowadays I have been known to call the shots on our dinner plans, our TV choices, and our Christmas destinations.

Note from Jinny

ON REGRET

Recognize that your marriage was not a mistake—it was a learning experience. It is okay to look behind you every once in a while to remind yourself of where you were and where you are going, and to be proud of how far you have journeyed from that first day of your divorce. With each hardship, you have learned something new about yourself. Never look back and say, "If only I had never started this trek" or "If only I had never gotten married" or "If only I had been stronger, wiser, or more fearless." "If only" is a phrase of the powerless, the weak, and the fearful. And you, my friend, are none of the above. Look at how far you have already come! You have your life back in your own hands, and a whole future ahead of you to turn it into exactly what you've always wanted. You can see this as a failure or as a new start, and it's the latter that will ultimately make you feel better about yourself. So when you find yourself falling into regrets, remind yourself to turn every "if only" into an "I will."

3. *Cry*

*"Let your tears come. Let them water
your soul."*—Eileen Mayhew

Show me a woman who has not cried after a divorce, and I will show you a woman who has not healed. It doesn't matter what the circumstances of the divorce were. If you called for the divorce, if he did, no matter what, you have to let yourself cry. Divorce is a loss, and it should be mourned. You are saying goodbye to a life and a person, no matter how good or bad that life or that person may have been. It is a long and final goodbye, and that is never easy.

I will be honest. I cried a lot. I cried until my tears were dry, my eyes were puffy, and my head ached. And in an odd way, it felt good! After a good crying session, I always felt better. Sometimes I even put a sound track to it. I would put on a sad song, or tear-jerking movie, and I'd just let go. I became a bit masochistic. I even sat down and looked through every picture in our wedding album. Pictures of vacations together, Christmas, pregnant . . . That might not have been the greatest idea. But why not? I let it all out! I enjoyed every second of it, because I knew that I had to go through it to feel better. I could have hidden my feelings, started going out before I was ready, and kept myself occupied with other activities, but no! I chose crying so that I could feel every single piece of the hurt and then move on.

I remember the exact day, the exact moment, when I decided I was going to stop crying—or at least stop crying so much. I was sitting in bed in the middle of the afternoon, and Jinny was with Cristian in the other room. I had either just started crying, was in the middle of crying, or had just finished crying. I heard the pitter-patter of my three-year-old's feet, and I tried to compose myself before he reached my bedside. I failed. "Mommy, are you crying again?" He looked at me, earnestly, just as I had looked at him so many times when he was upset, and he repeated the words I so often told him, "Don't cry. . . . It's going to be . . . fine!" And that was it. It was as if he had thrown me a rope. It was right there and then that I realized that my little boy was right: Everything *was* going to be fine. I had two precious boys, who needed me, and having them is the single-most important aspect of my life. Everything else would be just fine.

Note from Jinny

ON CRYING

Allow yourself to cry; you will always feel better afterward. Crying is a normal physical and emotional reaction, and it will help you heal. The emotions that you are experiencing during traumatic times are so heavy that your body cannot handle them. Crying is a behavior/reaction that helps you get in touch with the reality of the situation. You are connecting your mind and emotional self with your practical and physical self. It is often present in the acceptance process, when you realize that the divorce is actually happening and there is no going back. There are many reasons why you are crying, such as fear of this new change in your life, pain because the person you loved so much will not be by your side anymore, or the feeling of loss. For whatever reason (or reasons), you need to accept the reality of the situation and start looking to your future and the future for your family. Crying will help you experience that pain and start the healing process.

4. *Laugh*

Crying is much easier than laughing. It comes more naturally, more frequently, less forcefully. It's the laughing you have to work at. But it will come. Laugh at yourself, because let's be honest. You did some crazy things. And some ridiculous ones too! Or at least I did. Being crazy makes it easy to laugh at yourself later. After the divorce was final, I remember going off to look for my veil. I don't even know why I wanted it, but I remember being upset when I realized it was nowhere to be found. How does someone lose a twenty-foot veil? But the better question is, Why did I even care that it was lost? What was I going to do with it? Give it to Goodwill? Make it into a Halloween costume? What a nut I am! (But seriously, I do hope it did find it's way to a good Halloween costume. That was an intense veil, and it deserved a second life!)

And if you really want to know how crazy I am, I'll tell you the story I laugh at most. When we got married, we had a spontaneous civil ceremony in Vegas. Vegas was not part of my plan. I was the teenage girl who planned out the style of my wedding dress, what my chapel would look like, and how I would wear my hair. But there I was, in a hotel suite in Vegas, wearing a decidedly untraditional wedding dress, and worst of all, my hair was curly. My hair wasn't supposed to be curly! And this is the little detail I decided to flip out about—not the fact that I was getting married, but that I was getting married with curly hair! My soon-to-be husband turned to me and said, "What's the matter?" And I swear to you, I almost stopped the whole freaking wedding because my hair was not flat ironed. Two years later, in Puerto Rico, we renewed our vows in an amazing ceremony that was closer to my teenage vision (enter the twenty-foot veil), and believe me, I made sure my hair was just how I wanted. A year after that, we got separated and later divorced. So maybe the perfect hair isn't the key to marital bliss? But laughing at your crazy self just might be the key to postmarital bliss; eventually, it will help you get up off the couch, look in the mirror, and realize that maybe, just maybe, you should wash that poor hair you so crazily obsessed about. . . .

Laughing about things that once seemed so grave and important has been for me the best of remedies. When we are stressed or sad or worried, we tend to blow things out of proportion, and even the simplest detail (a hairdo, a veil) turns into something monstrous. Laughing about these things, about things that used to feel important but that have now lost their meanings or relevance, is the best way to diminish their hold on us. When something is laughable, it's trivial and therefore easier to overcome.

Note from Jinny

ON LAUGHING

Although it is hard to do, regardless of the stage you are in, try to think about the good times you experienced with your partner. This will help you stop blaming the other person and realize the reality of the situation. Understanding that this is a moment that you all need to go through, and although it's hard to see, everything will work out. You need to find old and new ways to laugh and enjoy life. Laughter will help you be able to see the light at the end of the tunnel and hope for your new life and the future.

5. *Rely on Others*

It is a sign of strength to know when to rely on others. This is not the time to be proud and pretend that "you can do it on your own." You cannot and you should not. But here is the key: You have to be discerning enough to surround yourself with positive friends and family. You do not need people who are going to tell you what to do or who are going to engage you in speaking ill of your ex. You need friends and family who are going to be able to pick you up when you are down and who are going to be able to pinch-hit for you when you are unable.

My support team includes:

Mom and Jinny: I was so vulnerable and at times I was not strong enough to be the mother that my children deserved. I recognized this and was lucky enough to have my mother and sister to rely on; they were always there to fill in when I was unable. They provided the patience and the strength for my boys when I could not. I also, as you know, relied on Jinny for my therapy.

My brother-in-law, Jose: Jose served as an amazing father figure for the boys when I felt so responsible for turning their world upside down. Seeing Jose with the boys made me feel less guilty about taking my sons' father figure away, since I realized that there are so many different types of father figures. Their uncle Jose will always be one of their great role models; I have tried hard to introduce into their lives other male figures who live up to the standard Jose set.

My brothers: My brothers were both in Puerto Rico at the time of my divorce, but each time I called them, they had me laughing in the first few minutes of the conversation. They had this way of putting everything in perspective, as older brothers often do.

Dad: Just hearing my dad's voice on the end of the line would make me feel as though I could let loose and cry all I wanted. The poor man. He never tried to stop me; he just let me cry. It felt so good just to let it all out and to know that I could, because Dad was strong enough to just listen.

My friends: Having friends to go shopping with, meet for coffee, or go to the gym with was so necessary for me. I just wanted to chat, get out of the house, not talk about the divorce all the time, and get my mind off of things.

Note from Jinny

ON RELYING ON OTHERS

In situations like this, people want nothing more than to make you feel better; however, regardless of their good intentions, sometimes they cannot give you what you need. You have to be aware of how certain people are making you feel when they are around you. It is up to you to surround yourself with family and friends whom you can rely on to help you move forward and support you through the stages you are going to experience. For example, if you have a very good friend who keeps telling you what a jerk your ex-husband is, and she draws you into afternoons of gossiping and bad-mouthing, be conscious of how this leaves you feeling. Do you really feel better once she leaves and you are standing there thinking about all she has said and re-hashing all of the bad times? I doubt it. Be aware that this is not going to help you move toward recovery. This does not mean that you cannot meet her for coffee or to go shopping, but do establish ground rules. Tell her, "Let's not talk about my divorce or my ex-husband. I am here with you to have fun and to get my mind off of it."

You must take time to identify who is going to help you, and it's okay to be a little selfish. You have to keep your best interests at heart. I remember when I went into labor, I knew who was going to help me get through it (my sister) and who was going to make it a little harder (my mother). I love my mother to death, but when there was a complication in my delivery, she began panicking and crying, and I knew that she was not going to help matters. I turned to Yari, who was calmly holding my hand, and I mouthed the words, "Get her out." Yari let go of my hand, put on a soothing CD, gently moved my mother into the hallway, and then came back to my side. I love Yari and my mother just the same, but I was in pain and I needed to put myself first. This is *allowed.* When you are in pain, there are going to be times when you have to put yourself first to get through it.

Be selective of whom you turn to for help, and make sure you choose the right person for the right time. It's not that you don't love all your friends. It's just that there are some who will be able to support and guide your more efficiently than others, and those are the ones you need to turn to. Remember, it's time for you to be a bit selfish and look out for exactly what you need.

6. *Trust Yourself*

"Trust yourself. You know more than you think you do."—Dr. Spock

I think I made a few really good decisions when I went through my divorce, though I don't know how. Perhaps it was beginner's luck. But mainly, I think it was because I trusted a deeper gut feeling. I really do believe that my subconscious mind led me through a lot of my decision making, because I can tell you that my conscious mind was in no state to be making sound judgments. I was walking around in a fog, but all the while I knew that I wanted to decide what was going to happen during my divorce. I knew that if I blindly followed the advice of others, I would regret it. At the time, I suppose it would have been easier to let everyone around me tell me what to do. I suppose it would have been easier to follow their advice. But if I had taken this route, I am sure I would regret it today.

For example, one of the "helpful tips" people kept giving me was to "take him to the cleaners'." "But at what cost?" I always asked. I think the smartest decision I made during my divorce was to be fair in the divorce proceedings, for three reasons:

1. I did not want to establish a toxic relationship with my ex. The last thing I would want is to be enemies with the father of my

children, and I think that there is no surer way to make an enemy than to get into a long, drawn-out legal battle over money, homes, cars, etcetera.

2. Spending time in a long, drawn-out legal battle over money, homes, and cars costs a lot of time and money that I would prefer to spend on my kids and not my lawyers. Instead, my ex and I decided to skip the fighting and be fair with each other. I knew in my heart that I would never be comfortable demanding an inordinate settlement. Because of our two sons, the relationship between my ex-husband and me will have to continue forever. Therefore I didn't want to start it off with a feeling of resentment and hatred, no matter how much pain I was going through at the time. We needed to reach an agreement that was fair for our children and that we were both happy with.

3. I can make my own money, thank you very much. I asked for what I thought was fair so that I could get back on my feet and still give my children a comfortable life. I do not need a huge alimony and child-support check every month. I needed to go back to work and prove to myself that I could provide for myself and my children.

Note from Jinny

ON TRUSTING YOURSELF

Understand that we are all great sources of energy and our job is to find happiness in this life. You are strong enough and smart enough to realize that your happiness is no longer possible if you continue to stay in your marriage. The fact that maybe "the love of your life" was not meant to be by your side for your entire life does not mean that you cannot still trust yourself. Divorce is a confidence-shattering experience, and you are likely to start questioning all of your decisions. This is perfectly normal; however, throughout this process, you need to start reconnecting with yourself and begin to trust your own instincts again.

You need to look at this as both a confidence-building and learning experience. The fact that your marriage didn't work doesn't mean that getting married to this man was a bad decision. The relationship changed, and you were strong and smart enough to realize that your happiness was more important than staying in a not-so-great marriage. This knowledge will allow you to remember the good times with your partner. It will allow you to understand that your marriage was in fact a good decision, but that you and your partner are not meant to be together any longer because your relationship is not what it once had been. With this knowledge, you can go forward and realize that you can trust yourself again.

7. *Respect Your Ex*

"You cannot respect yourself if you are not respecting others."—Anonymous

You don't always have to like your ex, but it is important to respect him throughout the divorce. It is so easy to fall into that trap of proclaiming him "the enemy." It is almost expected and accepted for ex-wives to hate their ex-husbands. I was in the un-fortunate position of being placed under a microscope by the press in the days, weeks, and months after my divorce. Journalists con-tinually asked me questions in the hope that I would answer by bad-mouthing my ex-husband. I knew what they were doing and why they were asking certain questions, and I was very careful not to say anything that could have been misconstrued. I wanted to maintain a level of mutual respect during our divorce so that we could continue to have a healthy relationship for the sake of our children and for our own sake. When I see ex-spouses who respect each other, I admire how mature and healthy they are. I always look to these couples with a certain sense of awe and ad-miration, mainly because they are the exception and not the rule. I have tried to be a woman who others could look to and say, "Look how gracefully she dealt with her divorce. Let's try to do it that way."

Note from Jinny

ON RESPECTING YOUR EX

What is our first response when someone is disrespect-ful to us? Most likely, we get upset, we build up a wall of protection, and we become disrespectful right back. This creates a cycle of blame, resentment, and hurt feelings. Each time the cycle repeats itself, the two par-ties fortify their walls of protection and become blind to their own roles in the conflict. This is true in all relationships, but in a divorce situation, the cycle is exaggerated. The ex-husband and ex-wife will hurt each other over and over again, and feel fully justified in doing so, claiming, "He hurt me, so I can hurt him," or "She did that, so I can do this." Clearly, the cycle of hurt is going to be harmful to both you and your ex. You have the power to change this to a healthy cycle, simply by acting with respect toward your ex (no matter how he is acting toward you). Act with maturity and respect, and in time a cycle of maturity and respect will be set into motion. It boils down to that old Golden Rule, which we all tell our children, but sometimes forget to follow ourselves: Do unto others as you would have them do unto you.

8. *Commit to Yourself*

"A dame that knows the ropes isn't likely to get tied up."—Mae West

For so long, you shared a life with someone and most of your decisions were tied to his decisions, his opinions, his likes and dislikes, and his schedule. Now, all of a sudden, that person is gone, and you will most likely feel lost and alone in the initial stages of your divorce. I know I did. It was still so hard to get out of bed some mornings. I felt overwhelmed by the fact that everything was on my shoulders. All of the decisions concerning my children, myself, and our future were entirely up to me. It overwhelmed me to the point of paralysis. But there did come a day when I said enough is enough—the day when Cristian came into my room and said, "Mommy, are you crying again?" I was embarrassed, and I knew that I did not want my sons to see me so sad all the time. From that day forward, I began to at least try to be positive and present in the my own life.

Admittedly, I was not very positive during this initial phase, but at least I started to see the light! My real breakthroughs came during the following two phases of Rebuilding and Rediscovery, but at this point I first admitted to myself that I was no longer happy in my marriage. Then I told myself that this was a fresh new opportunity and to take charge. Instead of saying, "Oh, no, I have to make all of the decisions," I said, "Wow, I can make all of the decisions!" I started to think about what I wanted out of this new life. Did I want to remain in Miami? Did I want to move somewhere new? Did I want to restart my career? And if so, how? What were my new priorities now that a huge priority of mine was gone? I turned all these painful questions into opportunities for empowerment, which slowly helped me change my perspective on the whole situation.

I did not answer any of my own questions in this phase. I allowed myself to pose questions, but I did not demand answers just yet. There would be time enough for answering to myself later.

Note from Jinny

ON COMMITTING TO YOURSELF

With a divorce, life gives you the opportunity to reevaluate your priorities, rethink your future, and seek out your own happiness. Your main purpose in life is to find happiness; admitting that your marriage was no longer making you happy is your first step in committing to yourself. It's not easy to admit something so painful, and it probably feels more like a gigantic leap than a step. But the good news is that every move you make after this leap will be easier and less scary. So after that first leap, take your time. Analyze where life has taken you and where you want to go.

It is critical that you be honest when you are analyzing these two factors. Once you understand where life has taken you and where you want to go, you can begin a healthy relationship with yourself. This is the most important relationship to foster in the early stages of divorce, because only after you have a healthy relationship with yourself can you have healthy relationships with others. A wonderful by-product of this self-recommitment is that not only will you be able to enter into new, healthy relationships, but many of your old connections (with your children, your family, your friends) will become even stronger than they were before.

9. Believe That Life Is Fair

"I have found that if you love life, life will love you back."—Arthur Rubinstein

It doesn't seem fair, does it? You dreamed of the fairy tale, the knight on the white horse, the castle. And then all of the sudden, poof, it's gone. The knight has left the premises, the castle has lost its grandeur, and you are sitting alone, wondering when your fairy tale marriage went haywire. Well, my friend, the fairy tales lie. They never give you the facts on marriage. Here are just a few:

Fact #1: The perfect marriage does not exist. As the French say, "There is no perfect marriage, for there are no perfect men." I have always loved the French.

Fact #2: You are not the first person to get divorced; you will not be the last. And yet in that moment of inexplicable sadness, you actually don't care about this fact. You care about your situation, and you are convinced that your divorce is the most traumatic event in the history of the world.

Fact #3: It is not. There have been world wars and plagues that have your divorce beat by a country mile. And yet I'm sure you don't care about this fact either. I certainly didn't.

Fact #4: Not everything ends in "Happily Ever After." Sometimes the chapter ends with "You will land on your feet." And you will. Maybe you've been bucked off of that white horse, or maybe you've been thrown, or maybe you've jumped. If you're like me, you landed flat on your face. My feet had nothing to do with the equation. I took baby steps, and today I am brave enough to take huge leaps. All. By. Myself. And you know what? I stumble every once in a while, but I really do always land on my feet. You will too.

Fact #5: Life. Is. Fair.

Note from Jinny

ON BELIEVING THAT LIFE IS FAIR

It is a trite but true saying: *There is a reason for everything.* Maybe at the time of the divorce, you don't understand why this is happening, but with time and patience, it will become clear. Even when we don't have all the answers to our questions, and everything seems uncertain, the only thing we know for sure is that *life is fair*. Things happen for a reason, and there is always—I mean, always—a silver lining to every situation. If you are a good person and work hard toward finding your happiness, life will support you and throw ropes along the way. Yes, change is hard, but it can also be extremely beneficial.

10. Embrace Life

*"What the caterpillar calls the end
of the world, the master calls the butterfly."*
—Richard Bach

Start with smiling. People will leave you alone for a little while if you force a smile every now and again. But be prepared. Soon they are going to try to get you to smile more often, to laugh, and eventually to leave the house (damn them, they mean well, but still damn them). I'll admit that the last thing I wanted to do was go out and be social. I just didn't want or need the looks of pity and the strained attempts to cheer me up. I was just fine being glum, thank you very much. But my friends kept saying, "Let's go bowling!" And my family kept saying, "Let's have a barbecue!" And I went bowling. And I made cameos at the barbecues, but I was really so much happier being miserable, alone in my room. I was being stubborn and a bit selfish, which I think is allowed. But at a certain point, you have to get on with it and let yourself embrace life. Get out into the world again. Meet people, interact, feel alive. It does a lot for your soul. It also helps to put the situation in perspective. Life is going to go on, and you are going to be fine, just as the great Cristian said. So let yourself love life, and life will love you back.

Note from Jinny

ON EMBRACING LIFE

I've said it before, and I'll say it again (just in case you weren't listening), your only responsibility in life is to be happy. Life will give you the opportunity and the time to find your own happiness, but it is up to you to take advantage of this. You need to be ready to handle the changes in your life. You don't have to be ready to handle it all. You don't have to know it all at the beginning. But you have to let yourself start. Understand that this is a process where learning and changes should be expected. You need to take control of your life and embrace it with joy. This is a new and exciting chapter in your life. Enjoy!

Final Words on Acceptance

At the beginning of my divorce, I perceived Acceptance as the great finish line at the end of the race. Then I got there and found out that it is only the beginning. Oh, for heaven's sake, you're thinking, who wants to run another marathon when she's just stumbled across the finish line, tired and out of breath? But once you get to this Acceptance stage, God gives you new life. The race will be different, because you'll get a burst of oxygen and fresh legs, and here is when you will find that you can open up and run. Okay, maybe you're ready to walk. I guess you have to walk before you can run. So stride briskly out into the sun, head up, legs shaven, and wearing something other than pajama pants. . . . The running will come later.

Part Two

Rebuilding

Putting the Pieces Together

"Remember, if you ever need
a helping hand, it's at the end
of your arm."
—*Audrey Hepburn*

*S*o there I *was: walking,* somewhat respectably dressed, legs shaven, and unbelievably overwhelmed. It was only months
ago that I was buried under the rubble. I had only recently
managed to dig myself out and come to terms with the divorce.
And now, as I walked around the remains of my past life, I realized that I had to rebuild a new castle. All by myself! My Lord,
I didn't even know where to begin, but I knew that I no longer
wanted to be paralyzed by this divorce. I didn't want to keep walking in circles around the wreckage. So with a baby on my hip and
a toddler grasping my leg, I began the trek forward the best way
I knew how: baby steps.

My first baby step was to start being present at the barbecues
that my family held at my house every Sunday. For months after
my divorce, Mom, Jinny, my brother-in-law Jose, and Jose's big
Colombian family would come over to my house to have Sunday
barbecues. They were doing it for my sake, I knew, but I could

barely muster the strength to make a brief cameo. I would pick at a few chicken wings, try to smile for everyone else's sake, and then head back to the cave of my bedroom. Then, one Sunday, after months of being in my bedroom, I forced myself to stay for the entire Sunday barbecue. I ate my fair share of wings and drank more than my fair share of coquitos, a traditional eggnogesque cocktail. I smiled and I may have even laughed, but I didn't do it for anyone else's sake this time. I did it for myself.

A few Sundays later, I started taking charge of the barbecues. I made the plans, called everyone to tell them when to come over, laid out the food, and chose the CDs. It felt so good to finally be taking charge of something. It felt so good to be around other people because I wanted to be there and not because people wanted me to be there. From organizing the Sunday barbecues, I gradually started to make plans to fill my Mondays through Saturdays. I joined the gym and took the boys to movies, the mall, or the zoo. I tried to do anything to get myself out of the house and into the world. And then, a little too early, a few months after separating from my ex-husband, I wanted to believe I had fully recovered. I wanted to say I was fine and happy again. After all, I had reentered society. I was wearing real people clothes and going out at night—if only to drive to my friend's house to talk—but at least I was getting out. So when I was asked to appear on a friend's talk show and talk about my future and my new career goals, I was excited. My intent was to go on the show and explain how the separation had made me stronger and more secure, and how excited I was for the future and the prospect of going back to work. In fact, most of the show would be about my career—the one I used to have and was working to rebuild.

Well, of course, the cameras started rolling, the divorce questions came, and you can guess what happened. I completely broke down. I was not ready at all. I had not recovered at all. All of my strength abandoned me, and I just started bawling. During each commercial break, I would think, "Okay, get it together. Be strong." But I never did get it together that day. I just was not ready. Driving home from that interview, I had two ways to look at it: I could be upset by my on-camera breakdown, or I could use it as an eye-opener. I let myself be upset for a day, and then I got over it. I used it as an eye-opener to realize that I was just not ready. I got up the next morning, and I chose to move forward, and that is how I got to where I am today, by waking up and deciding to move forward. Yes, there were days when I didn't want to move at all. But I put myself in the shower anyway, and I got out of the house, and I took the boys to the mall, the zoo, the movies. I gained a lot of my strength from those outings with my boys. I would run into friends and strangers who would say, "You look amazing," or, even better, "Your boys are so polite," and I cannot tell you how much that helped me, because I knew that I had arrived at this place all on my own. I looked "amazing" because, having forced myself out of the house, I was beginning to feel amazing. And my boys were "so polite" because I had instilled that in them (so I felt I must have been doing something right).

The most difficult part about the Rebuilding phase for me was that at some point I had to put the babies down in order to do it correctly. I had to put everything and everyone else down too. I could not keep filling my days to get my mind off of the situation. I had to face the situation and start to reevaluate my goals. If I was going to do this the right way, I had to give myself time alone to find out who I really wanted to be. Jinny kept telling me, "You have to be a little selfish. It's okay. This phase is all about you." But I had just spent years of my life stuck in a state where I let nothing be about me. I was a wife and a mother first. And nothing came before or after that. I allowed myself to be defined not by who I was, but by who everyone expected me to be. I never realized that letting yourself be defined in these terms—as the perfect wife and the perfect mother—is, ironically, the worst thing you can do for your marriage and your children. You have to stay strong, stay independent, stay true to yourself. Only then can others fully depend on you.

Go ahead, read that last paragraph again. Read it several times if you have to. Do you know how many times Jinny told me this before it sank in? Before I could even begin moving through this phase, I had to absorb the fact that I was going to have to be consciously selfish. It took me a few months to realize this. I wanted to fill all of my days going places with the boys and keeping my mind off of the divorce, instead of giving myself time to be alone and really think about what was happening. But Jinny kept after me to be a little selfish, and once I relented, she outlined the three stages of Rebuilding for me:

STAGE I. Forgive Yourself

STAGE II. Define Your Authentic Self

STAGE III. Identify Your Own Needs

I was a bit more confident in my ability to move through the stages this time. I had just conquered the Acceptance phase, and I felt as though I was finally on my way. I no longer felt guilty every day. I no longer felt angry or pained every day. Yes, the feelings crept up on me at times, but mostly I felt very proud of how far I had come. I could feel the change taking place inside of me. I could see how I was able to take more charge of my life. Whereas I once did not want to leave my bedroom for days, I was now waking up eager to get out of the house. But Jinny was right. I had to stop, take the time to get my thoughts in order, and rebuild my sense of self.

As instructed, I put everything and everyone else down, and I picked up a notebook. I started making lists, outlining my goals, and making plans for the future. I did not hold myself to these lists. If one of my goals sounded impossible, I wrote it anyway. I did not even try to act on these lists. I just let them be. Rebuilding is not about climbing the mountain; it is about laying your own foundations, and slowly and steadily building on top of these foundations. Later on, I would prioritize, go after what I wanted, and start climbing. For now I was content to pick up my notebook and walk forward.

Note from Jinny

ON REBUILDING

The Rebuilding phase is all about *you*. When you go through a divorce, everything in your life is thrown into disarray. You will feel as though the life you have created and worked so hard to achieve has been shattered. Think of it as a puzzle. When you are married, it seems that most of the pieces are in place and the picture is pretty clear. Then when you get a divorce, it is as though an earthquake or a hurricane has blasted through your pretty puzzle. Some of the pieces fly away, never to be found again. Others are broken in half. Very few, if any, remain where they were. It is up to you to pick up the remaining pieces and find new pieces that will fit into your new puzzle. This is very hard to do, if you are constantly focused on everyone else. You have to focus on yourself and decide what parts of this crazy mess you want to throw away, re-configure, or restore, and what new elements you have to add to the picture. The only way to do this is to drop everything else and begin reorganizing your big, mixed-up picture.

You are on a roller coaster of emotions, and your confidence and self-worth seem nonexistent at times. In the Rebuilding phase, you have to stop the roller coaster and return to a state of equilibrium. Focus on yourself, and let yourself go through the stages of Rebuilding completely. Let yourself be utterly selfish when you move through each stage; this is the only time you are going to be allowed, so take advantage of it!

The Stages of Rebuilding
Forgive Yourself . . . Define Your Authentic Self . . . Identify Your Needs

STAGE I: *Forgive Yourself*
"Without forgiveness, there is no future."—Desmond Tutu

I was horrible at forgiving myself. It was much easier for me to offer my forgiveness to others and then hold on to a piece of my pain and guilt. As much as I tried, I could not put down the pain and the guilt from the Acceptance phase, and yet I was determined to move on and rebuild, because I didn't have the time to wallow in my pain and guilt. So I took them along on the

Rebuilding journey. And then a magical thing happened. I realized that I was never going to be able to rebuild a strong foundation if I was constantly holding the guilt in one hand and the pain in the other. I realized that my life had become just that: the pain and the guilt. If I wanted to recover it, I was going to have to find the way to let go. I finally understood that until I forgave myself fully for everything that had happened, I was never really going to be able to offer my complete forgiveness to anyone. As hard as it is to do, you have to give yourself this forgiveness, because it is the key that frees you to move forward and rebuild.

As in the Guilt stage, I began to ask myself questions. But in the Guilt stage, I was a bit hard on myself. I asked: Was it all my fault? How could I do this to my children? And how could I take away my sons' father figure? This time around, I was kinder. I asked: What can I do to forgive myself? How do I let go of past mistakes? And how will this make me stronger?

1. What can I do to forgive myself?

The first thing I did was stop beating myself up. I told myself, it was okay. I reminded myself that circumstances and situations in my marriage were beyond my control, and I had done the best that I could at the time. For a while, I felt that every step I took in my marriage, I should have taken the other way. I told myself that if I did it all again, I would have done it all differently. But I probably would not have. I would have done it all exactly the same, because I didn't know any better. I know better now. So after I stopped beating myself up, I started being honest with myself and I asked:

2. How do I let go of past mistakes?

Did I make mistakes? Absolutely. But was it all my fault? Absolutely not. Humans make mistakes, especially when they are stuck in stressful situations, and a not-so-happy marriage is an incredibly stressful situation. You often feel that you can barely breathe or move in the thick, tense atmosphere of an unhealthy marriage. You are not yourself. Of course you are going to make a few mistakes. Do not let go of those mistakes. Learn from them. Take every little mistake and make it your ally. Were you too demanding? Too passive? Did you try to control everything? Did you allow yourself to be controlled? Recognize this about yourself. Admit this to yourself. If you are honest, you will be able to stop yourself from making these mistakes again, and you are ready to answer the question:

3. How will this make me stronger?
I had never felt as strong as the first day I decided to forgive myself. By forgiving myself, I was able to shed the victim mentality and I took back control of my life. When I was constantly blaming myself, I never felt secure or stable enough to move forward. When I finally let go of all my self-doubt and self-blame, I regained my footing and reclaimed my spirit.

When I faced the forgiveness stumbling block, and I responded by asking myself, "How will this make me stronger?" I knew that I was on the road to recovery. I decided to ask myself this question at every future setback, because it helped me to keep my focus on the future.

I asked myself more questions that pertained specifically to my situation. I encourage you to do the same. These three questions are great to start with, but do not stop here. Ask yourself as many questions as you need to in order to finally forgive yourself.

Note from Jinny

ON FORGIVING YOURSELF

Forgiving yourself is crucial to move on with your life. When you forgive yourself and those who have hurt you, you let the anger and pain out of your system, leaving the room to breathe and move on with a new and great chapter in your life. When you forgive, you are not necessarily forgetting. It is definitely okay and acceptable to forgive and still experience some pain because of it. Also, you don't hold anything against the person who caused the pain. . . . You just drop the heavy bag without turning around. Here are some steps that will help you achieve this important stage of forgiveness:

1. **EXPLORE YOUR FEELINGS:** Write your story in a journal. This will help you explore your feelings about the situation and obtain a clear sense of perspective. A journal or diary is a powerful tool; it forces you to communicate with yourself and be accountable to yourself, nobody else.

2. **WHAT DO YOU GAIN FROM IT?:** Remember that when you forgive, you are freeing yourself and preparing to move on with your life. This is your responsibility and nobody else's. It is up to you to stop carrying that heavy anger and pain. It is up to you to set yourself free. Nobody is capable of doing this but you. It is for that same reason that you are the only one gaining the most out of it.

3. **STOP AND TAKE A DEEP BREATH:** This is helpful when you are facing a challenging situation. Usually, when life presents a situation in which we are under stress, we forget to breathe calmly, creating a cycle where overwhelming emotions and an overstressed body do not connect. When you take your time to breathe in and out, you are allowing this connection to occur, giving yourself the opportunity to regain control—that same control we need to think, analyze the situation and come up with possible solutions to the problem. As my mom used to say, *"Tienes que pensar con cabeza fria"* (You need to think with a cool head).

4. **BE YOUR OWN HERO:** Think about the details of your story and use them as a power weapon to start controlling your life. After all, you are a strong person today because of all the experiences and lessons life has been giving you. When you allow yourself to forgive, you are definitely controlling your life. . . . You are becoming your own hero.

5. **ALLOW YOURSELF TIME:** Remind yourself that time is precious and very valuable. Give yourself the time to really repair the damage. Don't rush through it; live it and learn from it. After all, *"El tiempo es oro"* (Time is golden).

STAGE II: *Define Your Authentic Self*

"Make it thy business to know thyself, which is the most difficult lesson in the world."—Miguel de Cervantes

For so long I was defined by my two all-encompassing roles. I was my husband's wife and my sons' mother. While I took great pride in being a wife and mother, I lost a large portion of who I used to be. I had been an ambitious career woman, a dependable sister, a caring daughter, a fun girlfriend, and an all-around happy person. I would like to tell you that I was able to maintain these roles throughout my marriage, but the truth is, I did not. I recognized that that was my fault and that it was my responsibility to reclaim and redefine my authentic self.

I started out by forcing myself to answer the following questions as truthfully as possible:

Who am I today?
Who do I want to be?
What do I want to change about myself?
Why do I want to change these aspects of myself?
How am I going to change?
What are my strengths?
What are my weaknesses?

From these questions, I began to make lists:

My Goals:
My Rules for Myself:
My Most Important Values:

My Answers:

Who am I today?

Today I am fighting for happiness. I am stronger than I was yesterday, but not as strong as I will be tomorrow. I am divorced. I am a mother of two. I am very tired and sad, but I will be okay. I'm a little scared, but I'm on my way.

Who do I want to be?

I want to be the best mother I can be, and I also want to get back to work and have a great career. I want to be a mom, first and foremost, because it gives me more joy and happiness than anything I have ever done. I want to be a working woman, second, because it makes me feel strong and powerful to know that I can provide for my family and not give up a part that I once loved. I want it all, and I don't think it's as impossible as I used to.

What do I want to change about myself?

I want to get rid of the fear and the doubt. I want to be more assertive and less passive than I have these past few years.

Why do I want to change these aspects of myself?

I used to be fearless and doubtless, and I loved who I was back then. I want my sons to see me as this person, but I also want to see myself as this person again.

How am I going to change?

I will challenge myself, take chances, and make it a point to not always rely on others.

What are my strengths?

I am a great mom. I am caring, compassionate. I am a really good friend, daughter, and sister. I am fun and funny. I don't take myself too seriously. I never talk badly about others.

What are my weaknesses?

Sometimes I can be too nice and I let people walk over me. I have trouble sticking up for myself. I am not good at disciplining my sons, mostly because I feel guilt and I am trying to overcompensate.

My Goals

- I will raise two amazing sons.
- I will go back to work.
- I will learn to be firm with others.
- I will be kind to myself.
- I will appreciate my marriage and the lessons it taught me.

My Rules for Myself

- Stick up for yourself.
- Go with your gut.
- Be true to yourself.
- Start every day with a smile.
- Don't take life so seriously.

My Most Important Values

- Be kind.
- Be caring.
- Be truthful.

- Be happy.
- And above all else, be myself.

Note from Jinny

ON DEFINING YOUR AUTHENTIC SELF

You are your number-one project. As women, we are often told to put others first, and we come second, third, or last. Now I am telling you—*ordering you*—to put yourself first. In front of your family, your friends, your job, and yes, even in front of your children. You have to do this for yourself and for everyone else in your life so that you will once again be your best true self. But you can never again be that person if you don't let yourself be number one for a little while. If you have trouble, or if you start feeling guilty about putting yourself first, remember that you are doing it for others just as much as you are doing it for yourself.

The steps in the process of putting yourself first:

1. **DON'T BE SO HARD ON YOURSELF:** Wanting to be perfect is not always realistic. You do not need to put more pressure on yourself. Acknowledge, recognize, and praise the fact that you are surviving, breathing, and taking one step at a time. Take time to connect with your body and your mind. That connection is going to help you get your life under control again.

2. **YOUR FUTURE—THE LIGHT AT THE END OF THE TUNNEL:** Understand that everything happens for a

reason, you will be fine, and you have a future to build. Your future is your motivation and you need to commit to it. This commitment is going to give you the strength and the necessary tools to face what is happening to you at the moment. Your job is to keep that light as bright as you can.

3. **BE PRESENT ALONG THE WAY:** Regardless of the particular situation, you are exactly where you should be. Everything happening now, whether good or bad, is a necessary transition. You will be experiencing a lot of emotions and discoveries that will help you achieve your recovery. Take advantage of this opportunity and be honest with yourself.

4. **NOBODY CAN STOP YOU:** The main question is, *Who are you going to be?* This should be your priority, and you need to work hard to get exactly where you want to be. This is your time to grow as an individual.

5. **BE ALIVE:** One of the greatest gifts we have is the capacity to learn from our experiences. Life is not full of problems or failures; life is full of opportunities to learn from our actions and be better human beings because of that.

6. **IT'S OKAY TO FEEL FEAR:** What you are about to experience in this transformation can make you feel fear. Regardless of the source of the fear (maybe the changes, the unknown, the pressure, etc.), you need to be in tune with it and experience it fully. Understand that this is just the beginning to becoming the new you.

STAGE III: *Identify Your Own Needs*

"All I can do is be me, whoever that is."—Bob Dylan

After reviewing all of the lists I had made, I knew that three of the major needs that I had to address were:

1. Confidence
2. Competence
3. Self-Worth

I failed to address these needs during my marriage, and it was now up to me to reclaim them during my divorce. But how? For me, the answer was easy. I had to get back to work. I started my career at the age of seventeen, and a large sense of my confidence, competence, and self-worth stemmed from working hard and earning my successes.

I won Miss Puerto Rico at seventeen and Miss Universe at eighteen. I had never dreamed of being in one of these pageants. I was going to go to the University of Puerto Rico to study orthodontics. I had braces for eight years, so orthodontics became very interesting to me. At seventeen, when I was approached in the Plaza de Toa Alta to represent Toa Alta in the Miss Puerto Rico Pageant, I still had those braces. There was not always money to go to the orthodontist, but the pageant owners told me that they would pay for the rest of the treatment so that I would have a metal-free mouth in time for the pageant. That sounded good to me! So instead of the university, I was thrust into the universe, and I have never looked back.

As Miss Universe, I got to travel the world, be an ambassador for UNICEF, meet with foreign dignitaries and presidents of countries. I had never felt more confident in my life. After my one year as Miss Universe, I moved to the Philippines, where I hosted two weekly TV shows, starred in twelve movies, and created a charitable foundation for poor children. I stayed there for almost five years before I returned to Puerto Rico to record an album (*Dios mío,* please don't look for it). Though the album did well on the Billboard Dance Music Charts, I was not truly happy with the style of the music I was performing, so I decided to move to LA to pursue acting again. In March 1999, my friends took me to a club in Puerto Rico for a goodbye party, and that is where and when I met my future husband. So instead of moving to LA, I moved to New York, where he lived, and all of a sudden, I was out of my element.

Instead of focusing on my career, I focused on my relationship. We were engaged in October and married in May. We had our first child in February. Yes, nine months later, for those of you who are counting. No, it was not a shotgun wedding. Those of you who have children know that even if you find out early, you cannot possibly know you are pregnant until you are at least three weeks along! I found out about a month into our marriage, but it didn't stop the tabloids from having a field day with it. Anyway, back to the point. In a matter of months I went from being an actress and a model to being a full-time wife and mother. I loved it, but looking back, I realize that something was missing. I was not the kind of mother I wanted to be. Life had changed so drastically in such a short amount of time, and I did not slow down to consider my needs. Today, I am thankful that my divorce has given me the time to slow down, and in this Rebuilding phase I realized:

1. I needed a change.
2. I needed to go back to work.
3. I needed to be me again.

I wrote this down, content in the fact that I had identified these needs. It was not necessary (or wise) to start claiming these needs right away. Instead, I made plans. I was going to hire a manager, start auditioning again, maybe move to LA. It felt so good just to put these plans on paper. By identifying these needs and my plans, I started to see pieces of myself again. It only took me a few weeks before I reconnected with Jennifer, a friend in the business who became my manager. I started getting auditions right away and flying out to LA to take them. It was hard for me to leave the boys to take these auditions, and on a practical level, it was getting expensive. I began to seriously entertain the idea of moving to LA and started looking for apartments.

Note from Jinny

ON IDENTIFYING YOUR OWN NEEDS

Take everyone else out of the equation and understand that you are a human being and you have your own needs. You have to identify these needs in order to address them. Be honest with yourself. Many times after a divorce, women need to rebuild their sense of competence, their confidence, and their self-esteem. Ask yourself, what will help you do this? Do you need to go back to work? Get to the gym? Make a big move? Find new hobbies? Reconnect with old friends? Build new relationships? Ask the questions that you know will work for you. You are more in tune with your needs than you realize.

The Tools

Helping Yourself Rebuild

"There are no regrets in life.
Just lessons."
—*Jennifer Aniston*

This is the phase when I bought all of the *Sex and the* City DVDs (which I think is a necessary tool for any girl during this Rebuilding period), and I would let myself watch two or three episodes in a row. Okay, sometimes four or five. There was something so therapeutic about watching four beautiful single women talking about and tackling the grand issues of love and relationships. And often failing. If any woman tells you that she did not identify with Carrie, Samantha, Charlotte, or Miranda, I say she is lying. These four women, it seemed, were speaking to every other woman in America. Or at least I felt as if they were speaking to me.

I watched all six seasons in a matter of months, so I got to see the women go from relationship to relationship in fast-forward. It is really the best way to watch the show, since you realize that though the four women were constantly jumping from one romantic (or sometimes purely sexual) relationship to another, the whole show was about a woman's relationship with herself. So, when I heard Carrie utter those final words, "The most exciting, challenging and significant relationship of all is the one you have with yourself," I remember smiling to myself and thinking, "Okay, Yari, let's start dating." At that moment, I entered a relationship with myself that I took seriously. I had to do this relationship the right way. I could not settle for any less.

I made a point to add a few more tools to my bag, and I set out to build a relationship with myself. I knew I needed to make the foundation strong and rock solid; these six tools helped me to lay down the cornerstones and I built up from there. Again, feel free to steal each of these tools and add them to your own bag as you need them:

1. Clear Your Head
2. Let It All Go
3. Refocus
4. Reinvent Yourself
5. Empower Yourself
6. Have Courage

1. *Clear Your Head*

"Since everything is in our heads, we had better not lose them."—Coco Chanel

I could not fully focus on my own Rebuilding if I did not constantly clear my head. One of the most challenging parts of divorce is that life keeps on going. There are no "time-outs" on account of your divorce. The air conditioner will break if it feels like it. The car will just stop running. A song that sends you into a tailspin will come on the radio. Hurricanes will power on through without asking your permission. And you will probably have a breakdown or two. But that is why there are mornings. No matter what you are going through, no matter what curveballs are thrown your way, life will give you a fresh start every twenty-four hours.

I made it a point to use each morning as a time to clear my head and remind myself of what I wanted to do that day. I would think about all that I had written in that old notebook. I would recall all of the questions I asked myself. Who am I? Who am I going to be? I tried to clear everything else out and continually ask myself, Who do I *want* to be? I obviously knew that I wanted to be happy, healthy, and successful. But, true to my nature, I wanted to be *impossibly* happy, *impossibly* healthy, *impossibly* successful. I will tell you, there were days when I just could not see myself ever being the person I wanted to be. Yes, some days I could actually see myself being that insanely happy person again. Then some days I just felt insane. On these insane days I would remind myself that I could not slow down life, but I could slow down *my* life. I could stop, take deep breaths, and tell myself that it was going to take time.

I would take the boys to the park, or go to the gym, or start redecorating parts of the house, or take out my notebook and write. Sometimes I would just sit in the kitchen with Mom and Jinny. We would talk about everything and nothing in particular. Mom would make us a snack, just like she would when we were girls. As the smell filled the house, I would immediately feel at ease, and my worries would fade away. For me, there still is nothing more mind clearing than having Mom create the tastes and smells of my childhood. I cannot help but feel happy and incredibly blessed. I cannot help but remember where I come from and remind myself of where I want to go.

Note from Jinny

ON CLEARING YOUR HEAD

Your mind is your most powerful weapon; the battle starts here. All of your actions follow your thoughts, so you need to clear your head before you can act positively. Do not continue to berate yourself or cloud your thoughts with old regrets. Use your mind to see yourself as the person you want to be. If you consciously think in this manner, you will subconsciously act in ways that will help you to achieve this vision of a happy, healthy, and successful person.

2. *Let It All Go*

"The truth will set you free. But first, it will piss you off."—Gloria Steinem

I started to gain control of the present when I finally started to let go of my own personal demons. I would like to say that I left it all behind me in the Acceptance phase, but the truth is, I did not. I left behind the regrets, pain, and anger I had *toward the situation*, but I still carried around regrets, pain, and anger *toward myself*. I do think that I fully admitted the truth in the Acceptance phase, but I continued to have those nagging feelings that I should have done everything differently. Mostly, I kept wondering how I let everything get so out of control. How did I let myself become such a shadow?

I was so mad at myself, but I finally faced the truth: I do know how it happened and it was my fault. I had stopped taking responsibility for my own life. I can remember times, exact moments in fact, when I should have taken charge of the situation, but I did not. I recognized that I was not the woman I wanted to be, and yet I did not make any moves to change that. I wanted to go back to work. I thought that perhaps I could be in a few commercials or go on a photo shoot every once in a while; I knew it would boost my confidence and make me feel better about myself. I had the resources around me to do that. I had friends in the business who were more than willing to help me, yet I decided not to take the steps. I was too overwhelmed. Instead, I decided to sit on the sidelines for five years, halting my career, but even more important halting my growth as a woman.

Now, in this Rebuilding phase, I had a decision to make: I could either dwell on my past mistakes, or I could let it go and move on. I knew that dwelling on the past would eat up the present and cloud the future. That is not a cycle that I wanted to set in motion. Instead, I just let it all go. It took me a while and many hours of talking things through with Jinny. I talked about all of my regrets until I was blue in the face and there was nothing left to say. At that point, I was tired of walking around with this baggage, and when there was nothing left to say, I decided just to let go. All of my mistakes, all of my missteps, my regrets, my anger, my pain, I let them all go . . . and that is when I gained control.

Note from Jinny

ON LETTING IT GO

Understand that the past is over and done. You cannot change it. In the Acceptance phase, you let go of regret. In this phase, you let go of everything you cannot control:

1. You cannot control what you said or did during the marriage, but you can control what you say and do today.
2. You cannot control how your ex acts toward you, but you can control how you react toward him.
3. You cannot control what people are going to say about you, but you can control how you respond.
4. You cannot control the decisions you made before today, but you can control every decision you make from this day forward.

Confidence is related to control, and what you control now is the present and your actions. Forget what has happened and focus on the present and what you do control. Use the past to push you on into the present. Think about the lack of control you felt in the past and realize that you have the power now. You have control of the present and every day from now forward. This will help you to think about the endless possibilities when you think about what lies ahead.

3. *Refocus*

Focusing on the not-so-good times and wondering what I could have done to make them different was not going to help me to re-build. Instead, I chose to focus on those days that I felt extremely productive and proud of myself, and tried to re-create those days in my head. For example, I have always loved to redecorate. There is something about it that gives me an incredible sense of satisfaction. So I started sifting through my mind to find the moments in which such a simple thing as redecorating had made me feel important.

When Jinny was pregnant with her daughter, Andrea, I decided that I would design and decorate the nursery. Luckily for me, Jinny gave me free rein, and I went crazy. Or actually I took free rein. She kept saying, "What are you doing? Can't you tell me what you are doing?" And I said, "Back off, Jinny! If I had a daughter, this is how I would do her room." And she backed off, but mostly because she was about eight months pregnant, and if it came down to a fight, we both knew I could have taken her.

I did the room in a princess theme. I painted it soft pink and stenciled jewelry patterns around the top border. I made a crown canopy to go over the crib and painted a little frog prince in the corner. Above the light I stenciled the words BE-LIEVE IN YOURSELF. It took me about two weeks, and at the end, I was delighted! Besides the fact that I had designed the most magical baby girl room I had ever seen (if I do say so myself), it took my mind off of the divorce and put my focus on something that I loved to do. It was then that I realized how powerful it was to refocus my energies on the positive and drown out the negative.

Note from Jinny

ON REFOCUSING

The best way to refocus on the positive is to recall the times when you felt most confident and satisfied with yourself. First, you can choose an activity that you know you are good at and make a plan to start a project that will give you a sense of satisfaction. Second, you can think about a specific situation or a specific day. Why was that day so special? What were you doing? Think about that day and work to reexperience that feeling. Get in touch with your thoughts, feelings, and actions on this day. Refocusing on the details of one great day can help you to open yourself to many more like it.

4. *Reinvent Yourself*

"Always be a first-rate version of yourself instead of a second-rate version of someone else."
—Judy Garland

I let myself explore and experiment to find out exactly who I wanted to be. I knew that I wanted to stay true to myself, but I also knew that I wanted to make some changes. After I built up my confidence, I allowed myself to find out what other aspects of my personality I wanted to foster. I outlined exactly the kind of mother, daughter, sister, and friend I wanted to be. Mostly, I wanted to be a better version of the girl I had been before I started my career. I used my divorce as a time to reflect on not just my marriage, but on the last ten years of my life. I was so young when I was approached in the plaza. I had not yet solidified my goals, my hopes, and my dreams. I was naive and idealistic and impressionable. I do think that I let myself be influenced in so many aspects of my life and my career. If people gave me advice, I would blindly follow, because I thought that they must know what they were talking about if they had been working in the business for so long.

I believe that I was so fortunate to have been given all of the opportunities that my career has offered, however a part of me feels as though I missed out really growing into myself. Most of my friends went to college and were given a fresh start at eighteen. I decided to stop and give myself the opportunity to do it at twenty-nine. I took time to find out what I wanted to do with the rest of my life. I made so many lists of my plans and dreams. (I am going to go to Paris and really *see* it. I am going to learn French . . . and Italian . . . and Portuguese. I am going to take violin lessons again. . . . The list goes on and on. . . .) I went after some of my dreams and plans right away, and some of them have been put on hold until my children are old enough to drive themselves to baseball practice. But they are all there, written in my notebooks, waiting for me to make them come true.

Note from Jinny

ON REINVENTING YOURSELF

Take this as an opportunity to learn a lot about yourself. Be aware of who you are and who you want to be. Be honest with yourself and do not neglect to identify areas of improvement. Do you need to learn to be more assertive? Easier on yourself? Nicer to yourself? Take advantage of this time to reinvent yourself and become the person you have always wanted to be. Think about your dreams and longings—the things that you had always wanted to do but somehow forgot along the way. Whether it's taking up skydiving, starting a restaurant, climbing Kilimanjaro or moving to a foreign country, give yourself the chance to change your life completely. Not many people have the opportunity to do this in their lifetimes, so no matter how painful your divorce may have been, learn to also see it as a blessing. Take responsibility for rebuilding a life that you are excited about living.

5. *Empower Yourself*

The one thing about being married is that you get used to deciding things and making plans as a team. I was so used to always consulting on every decision I made with my husband that once we were no longer together, I felt lost. For a long time, I would consult on everything with friends and family, in an effort to regain that additional support that I had grown so accustomed to. But as time went by, and I felt like I was slowly regaining control of my life, I realized that I was going to have to start making my own decisions—all by myself. I could not keep asking my friends and family for their input. It felt safe to have the cushion of reassurance from Mom or Jinny or a girlfriend. They could tell me that I was making the right move, and I took comfort in that. Yet I knew that I could not continue my life with this cushion. I knew that I had to kick it away sooner or later. Instead of sweeping it out from under myself right away, I decided to pull it away inch by inch.

I knew that I was not ready to make my big decisions just yet, so I let myself make the small ones at first. I'd take on any challenge that seemed tangible, anything I knew I could tackle and emerge victorious (decorating the boys' bedrooms). Then I allowed myself to take on the tougher adversaries. Slowly but surely, I started to notice how I was able to conquer every challenge I set myself up against, no matter how hard it had seemed at first. I remember looking around at my house one day, so proud at how it looked, and then realizing that I had done it all myself. The sense of accomplishment I felt at that particular instant was nothing short of what one must feel when standing at the top of Mount Everest: I went from not wanting to venture out of my bedroom to redecorating and reorganizing my entire home environment. I had challenged myself and conquered.

Another time I truly surprised myself was one day when I decided that I was going to take Cristian to Disney World, all by myself. Keep in mind, that I had barely done anything by myself during the past year. But this day, I put him in the car, drove four hours from Miami to Orlando, picked up his sister, and then the three of us went to Disney World. It was just the kids and me, and I finally felt capable and self-sufficient again. Making all of these seemingly small moves helped me build up my confidence, so when the opportunity arose, I felt strong enough to make bigger decisions (e.g., did I want to stay in Miami, where I was safe and comfortable? Or did I want to move to a new city, where I could continue to challenge myself?). It was by starting with the small stuff that I was eventually able to recapture my confidence in myself and realize what I could accomplish.

Note from Jinny

ON EMPOWERING YOURSELF

Your power is in the choices you make. The sooner you start making your own choices—both big and small—the faster you'll start to feel yourself regain control over your emotions and your life. One of the most frustrating things about going through a divorce is that feeling of powerlessness that often overwhelms women when they feel that their life plan has been taken away from them. But as soon as you realize that your life is still there and still yours to live, you will begin to feel much stronger and more powerful. You are responsible for your own choices and self-esteem. Don't wait for people around you to start giving you power, and do not let them make choices for you. As much as they may love you and care for you, nobody knows what is better for you than you. Whether it's the color you decide to paint your bedroom, or where you're going to live, every single decision you make will help you reconnect with who you are and what you want this spectacular new life of yours to become. Search yourself for what will make you feel empowered.

6. Have Courage

"Be brave. Take risks. Nothing can substitute experience."—Paulo Coelho

I did not always know what was coming around the corner, and at first this scared the hell out of me. But then I started to get a rush out of the walking into the unknown. I started to remember the crazy, courageous girl I had once been. When I was seventeen and traveling through Europe and Asia during my year as Miss Puerto Rico, I used to flit from country to country without a fear in the world. I had no money, no chaperone, no cell phone, and no language besides Spanish. Back then, the pageant did not give you a stipend, an entourage, or a translator. You were on your own, my dear! Today I think that maybe I should have been a little scared, but back then I do not think fear ever entered my mind. I was brave, because I gave myself no other option. Now, in the face of a new divorce, I had the money, the chaperones, and the cell phones. I could have relied on all these luxuries, but instead I decided to be that brave seventeen-year-old girl again. And I gave myself no other option.

In 2005, less than two weeks before the *Premio Lo Nuestro* Awards (the highest-rated Latin Awards TV Show), my manager received a call from the show organizers asking if I wanted to do a surprise flamenco number during a pop singer's performance. Without hesitation, I said of course I would do it. Looking back, I can say that maybe that was a little crazy. I had never flamenco danced before, but I committed myself to giving it my first shot on stage, at a huge televised award show. Ten days was enough time to learn the flamenco, right? It had to be, I decided. I was once again that strong, fearless seventeen-year-old girl who did not think twice about taking on a challenge. So almost two weeks after that phone call, I was up onstage in a packed American Airlines Arena in a bright red dress, dancing the flamenco. It was one of the most freeing moments of my life. I wasn't dancing for the crowd or for the cameras. I wasn't dancing for anyone but myself.

During my five years as a talk show host in the Philippines, I always had dance routines to learn for both of my TV shows. Dancing was my favorite part of work as a TV host because it was when I felt most free, most like myself. The people in the Philippines even starting calling me "the Dancing Queen" (a nickname that I am quite proud of, being a girl from Puerto Rico). Up on the stage that night, I again felt like the old Yari. I remember going backstage to see my friend and manager, Jennifer, who had been with me through all my ups and downs. She had tears in her eyes, and at that moment I realized that she felt it too. I had been reborn on that stage. Minutes later, after the dance, I walked out onstage again to present an award, and the crowd stood up and gave me an ovation I will never forget. I will forever be thankful to the people in the crowd that night, but mostly I realize that I should thank myself as well. I should thank myself for being brave and saying yes, because in essence I was saying yes to so much more. I was saying, "I am coming back and I am going to be me again," for I had decided only weeks before that I was going to accept my divorce as a clean slate. I was going to start over and be the happy, vivacious girl who knew how to bring down the house while dancing for nobody but herself. And dammit, that's what I did.

Note from Jinny

ON HAVING COURAGE

Do not withdraw from the challenging or painful obstacles of this Rebuilding phase. They are going to come, and they are going to threaten to break down all that you have been working toward. Remember the courage you have already displayed by making the decision to get out of an unhealthy relationship, despite all the societal and emotional pressures that entails, and apply this courage to all stumbling blocks you may face. Remember: All of the greatest hurdles are behind you; any hurdles ahead of you, you can handle.

Final Words on Rebuilding

Just as I was ready to walk, baby step by baby step, out of the Acceptance phase and into the Rebuilding phase, I was now ready to run, stride by stride, out of the Rebuilding phase and into my Rediscovery. I had just about enough of focusing on me. I like myself just fine, but constantly trying to investigate myself got exhausting! I wanted to get back out into the world and show it just what I had. I had been on the bench for far too long. So I took a deep breath, and I started to sprint . . . sail . . . fly. My eyes were focused on the horizon, and my heart was hungry.

Part Three

Rediscovery

Embracing Your Life

"Dance like nobody's watching;
love like you've never been hurt.
Sing like nobody's listening;
live like it's heaven on earth."
—Mark Twain

When I finally, finally reached the Rediscovery stage, I was so excited to sprint into the future. It was exhilarating, empowering . . . and hard. I know you are probably thinking, "Well, so far she has said that every step of this process is hard." I'm being honest with you; it is not a cakewalk. Every single part of the Recovery and Rediscovery period is hard. There have been days when I feel as though I am running full force and nothing can stop me. And then there are days when I hit a wall and need to give myself a rest. I am still experiencing these days, and I am savoring every single moment, the good and the bad. For so many years, I never let myself run full force, and I never ran out of breath trying to find myself. I let myself be somebody else entirely, a girl I barely knew, and the day I entered my Rediscovery phase was the day I was ready to find the old Yari again. Of course, I had no idea I was "entering my Rediscovery phase." I never knew I was entering any phases at all until I looked back and identified the "Aha!" moments. At this phase, my "Aha!" moment came in the form of a can of pink paint.

When I met my ex, I was a "pink paint" kind of girl. I was lively and eager to take on the world. I was studying Portuguese and learning to play the violin, I was going to take acting lessons, and best of all, I was going to move to LA. I had a whole list of dreams that I cannot even remember because I let them fly right out the window the moment I met him. I let my relationship become my life. And what happened to my prior life? I'm sorry to say it flew out the window with the Portuguese and the plane ticket to LA. And that, I can finally admit, was my fault. Why didn't I hold on to the violin as I fell head over heels? Maybe I wanted to let myself free-fall without anything to hold me back. But after almost a year of the free-falling, I finally landed in the reality of my marriage, and realized I didn't even know who I was anymore.

I was not working, I had let go of all of my hobbies, and I was living on Long Island, so far away from my family and friends. I had let my license expire. I would spend my days wandering around that large home, and I had never felt so poor, so lonely, so lost. I did not know what to do with myself. Just going into Manhattan to meet with my ob-gyn was an adventure. I would redecorate parts of the house, out of sheer boredom, and I was choosing grays and beiges, for God's sake! I was *never* the gray, beige girl, but that was the girl I let myself become. I went from bolds to neutrals in a matter of months.

For a long time, it was impossible for me to see how much of my personality and vivaciousness I had lost. I could not see this during the marriage or during its aftermath. It was only after I worked through all of the Acceptance and all of the Rebuilding, when I was watching Mom paint my bedroom a bright pink, that

I began to understand how far gone I was and how far back I had managed to pull myself. It may not have seemed like a big deal to anyone else, but it was a huge deal to me. Those pink walls meant so much more to me than I can tell you, and I did not stop there. I had mauve curtains, feathered pillows, gigantic daisies, pictures of Paris, and a huge portrait of Audrey Hepburn. It was such a girl's room. It was purely and perfectly me. I was quite proud of myself and my pink room. I was coming back to life. I also changed my hairstyle and colored my hair red—not my very best look. I started eating healthier and going to the gym. I went to the spa and got massages (Why hadn't I done that before?). I took the window seat in the airplane, instead of always deferring to the aisle. I reveled in the fact that the walk-in closet was all mine—all mine—and started taking my boys out on weekend outings. The point is, it took a pretty long time to get myself to a place where I began to notice my revival, but once I started seeing these small accomplishments, I felt so much better about myself. With my newfound confidence, I was ready to take on my bigger goals. I was on the road to full Rediscovery and I did not want to veer off of it.

After all of the Acceptance and the Rebuilding, all of the self-doubt and pain, I emerged from my bedroom and decided that I was going to take control of things. I set off on a mission not just to redecorate each room in the house, but to reorganize every corner too. The redecorating was fun for me, but the reorganization felt like a monumental task since it was really my conscious effort to take charge again.

When we finalized our divorce, I was living in a new house in Miami, and my ex-husband was living in our old house in New York. Everything of the boys' and mine was shipped down to the Miami house, and I mean *everything*. It was so overwhelming that at first I just wanted to leave the boxes in the garage and forget about them. I was overwhelmed by the sheer mass of it all, but also by the fact that it felt as though my entire marriage was packed away in those boxes. I just did not feel like opening it all up. Until one day, I felt like I had to open these remnants of my past if I was ever going to lay claim to my new life. It was painful to go through all of the boxes, but in an odd way, it was also therapeutic. I found myself passing down or donating the bulk of what had been shipped, not because I was bitter or cynical, but because I wanted to start fresh.

Everything that I saved I saved for a reason. I saved our wedding album and the video so that I could pass it along to my boys one day. I want them to see how beautiful the wedding was and how in love we were, and show them that they were the product of a wonderful, loving relationship. I saved our favorite photos; all the photos of the boys with their father cover the walls of their room so that they always know he is with them. These are the types of treasures I held on to. But more than anything, I just let go, and it felt so good.

Note from Jinny

ON REDISCOVERY

The Rediscovery phase is a phase that should never end; so it should actually work more like a cycle. These are not stages that you go through, but steps that you will constantly repeat each time you go after another goal.

STEP   I: Contemplate the Possibilities

STEP   II: Prepare for Change

STEP III: Take Action

STEP IV: Keep the Cycle Going

Whether after a divorce or at any point in your life, it is important to set goals for yourself, regardless of how big or small they may be. But it's also just as important to structure them in an organized way. The clearer you are in the way you are going to achieve these goals, the easier it will become to lead them to fruition.

STEP I: *Contemplate the Possibilities*

"The question isn't who is going to let me; it's who is going to stop me."—Ayn Rand, The Fountainhead

Faced with the prospect of reinventing a whole life ahead of me, I pulled out all of my old notebooks from the Rebuilding phase, and I flipped through to see all of the plans, dreams, and goals I had set for myself. Dios mío, did I have plans! I had some crazy pie-in-the-sky plans that I may still pursue. But there were three that I wanted to pursue right away, that I *had* to pursue right away. I wrote these three down, along with my motivations for setting these goals:

GOAL #1: START WORKING AGAIN

Motivation: No matter how awful it can be sometimes to have to wake up every morning and go to work, the truth is, it's an essential part of human life. You do something, you feel productive, and you're an active part of the world around you. I knew that it would make me happy, fill me with satisfaction, make me a better mother, and boost my confidence. During my marriage, working was definitely one of the things I missed most about my previous life. I had been acting, modeling, and TV hosting for seven years straight, and all of a sudden, I was doing nothing. I missed being around people and the happiness that came with working.

GOAL #2: MOVE TO LOS ANGELES

Motivation: Living in LA had been a dream of mine for years. This was where I was heading when I met my ex, but I put the dream on hold to move to New York. Every time I flew to LA (after the divorce) for a job or an audition, it just felt right. I felt at home, and what's more, I felt independent. I had to do this, not just for my career, but for my own well-being and for my sons.

GOAL #3: GO TO PARIS, SEE THE ENTIRE CITY,
AND RIDE A BICYCLE TO GO BUY BREAD.

Motivation: Just because! I had always wanted to do this! There was something about Paris that had always appealed to me, and I felt that at last it was time for me to go and see for myself.

Once I wrote down these goals and my motivations for setting them, I realized that I was addressing the three issues that I had been trying to improve upon throughout this whole process: self-confidence, competence, and self-worth. Going back to work would make me confident and sure of myself again. Moving away from Miami and everyone I knew would make me feel independent and competent again. And taking that trip to Paris and letting myself spend time and money on my own happiness was a way of letting myself know that I was worth it!

These were all pretty big, life-altering goals (at least the first two), and they were going to cost me a good deal of time and money if I wanted to pursue them. So, because I was no longer eighteen, because I had financial obligations, and because I had two children on my hips, I had to stop and really think about why I was going to go after these goals. Was I trying to prove something to myself (a valid reason), was I trying to prove something to others (a less valid reason), or was I running away from my pain (not a valid reason at all)? I also had to think about my future and see if these were goals I could live with for a long time. While going to Paris had no dire consequence on my life or the lives of those around me, going back to work and moving to LA did, and I had to think about that. I also had to sit down and think hard about whether my goals were realistic or not (there would be time for less realistic goals later, when the kids were grown, when I wasn't in such a transition phase, but for now, I had to be able to succeed). For each of my goals, I decided:

> *1.* Yes, I was doing it for myself.
> *2.* Yes, I would be happy with it in the future.
> *3.* Yes, I could realistically achieve it.

And that is when I solidified my three big goals, wrote them on a piece of paper, placed it on my bathroom mirror, and started making a plan.

Note from Jinny

ON CONTEMPLATING
THE POSSIBILITIES

This is the perfect time for you to close your eyes and envision the life you want to have. Take your time to think and analyze who you were before, who you want to become, and those desires you want to achieve. This is the time for you to start contemplating the idea of making changes and moving forward by yourself. At this time, commitment is not an issue; you just need to think and allow yourself to discover new equations between your options and those needs and desires you would like to fulfill in life.

Some of the questions that will serve as a screening process for your aspirations:

Is this goal in tune with my values and beliefs?
What are the costs and benefits of going for this goal?
What are the costs and benefits of not going for this goal?
Is this goal achievable?

It is important to recognize that when setting your goals, you need to make sure not only that they are consistent with your values but also that they are achievable. One of the hardest things you can expose yourself to is working really hard toward a goal that at the end is not aligned with your values and/or is not realistic for you. This will only create a sense of failure and interrupt the rediscovery process. Because of all the emotional changes you have been through, this can become a long and difficult process; you need to be aware and ready for it. Allow yourself time to navigate throughout your options and do not rush yourself. Although this is a very personal process, your family and friends can serve as a support, especially

> when you are having a hard time listing those goals
> and dreams that you might have stopped thinking
> about along the way.

STEP II: *Prepare for Change*
"Failure to prepare is preparation to fail."—Unknown

I am a girl who likes a plan, so once I had that list on my bathroom mirror, I started to prepare. The first goal, "Go Back to
Work," stared me in the face each morning, and each morning I
made small plans. Before I was married, I had a successful acting
career in the Philippines and Puerto Rico. Initially, I had planned
to parlay this success into an acting career in the United States
(which is why I was going to move to Los Angeles in 1999). Instead, I met my ex-husband, moved to New York, and focused on
being a wife and a mother. Now, five years later, I wanted to pick
up my career where I had left off, but the world does not make
that so easy, does it? We cannot hope to jump back into the game
after sitting on the sidelines for years. I was not naive; I admitted
this to myself and was realistic with my expectations. I knew that
it would take a lot of preparation, so I began by making a plan.

The first step in my plan was always to gather my resources
(which usually involved telling my family and friends my goal).
For example, when I decided I wanted to go back to work, I con-
tacted my old friends and colleagues, who I knew would bend
over backward for me. I also explained my intentions to all of my
family members, who I knew would be behind me 100 percent.
And believe me, having my friends' and family's support during
this first huge transition was essential. I knew that I could not do

it without them. It's hard enough to put yourself out there to find a job, so it always helps to know that there's someone you can call when you're feeling down.

For the second goal, moving to LA, my family in Miami was less enthusiastic, so I knew that they were not the people to talk to about the move. Although I informed them, of course, of what I was planning to do, I didn't seek their immediate support on this plan because I knew they didn't want it. But in LA I had great friends, who backed my decision, who were there for me when I landed, and even helped me go house hunting. These friends were the resources I needed to move to LA, and they were the ones who could help me make this process all the less difficult.

For my third goal, going to Paris, I made a plan with my good friend and photographer, Omar, who knows Paris inside and out, and I recruited him to come along on the trip with me.

I am sure that your goals are completely different from mine, but no matter what they are, it is important that you *prepare* for them. If there's one thing that I learned throughout this whole process, it is that while finding what your goals are is an important first step, it is completely useless if you don't prepare and seek out the people who will be able to help you achieve them. Otherwise your goal is just a far-off dream (e.g., me and my violin).

Note from Jinny

ON PREPARING FOR CHANGE

Change is not always easy. In order to be ready for change, you must identify your motivation. Your motivation is what will keep you going, especially during the challenging times. Write down your goals on a piece of paper and place the paper where you can see it on a daily basis (the bathroom mirror, the refrigerator door, etc.). This will serve as a reminder to move forward and as a source of strength. Then it is time to make an action plan and start gathering your resources:

1. **MAKE AN ACTION PLAN:** Making an action plan is as crucial as your commitment to apply it. The action plan is going to help you organize your thoughts and to divide your goal into small bite-sized pieces that are attainable. There is no use, for instance, to be a surgeon if you have no prior knowledge of the medical field. Achieving those small steps will keep you feeling at ease and motivated to move forward in the right direction. The feeling of success that you experience when achieving those small steps will fill you in with a great satisfaction that gives the strength to keep working on achieving your goal. It is always beneficial to think about some potential obstacles that you may experience when working toward that goal. But don't deal on the negative. Think about some solutions to overcome these obstacles.

2. **IDENTIFY WHAT YOU HAVE AND WHAT YOU NEED:** This is the time for you to know if there is any support or any skills you will need to achieve your goal. Support is always good when making a change. Seek

support from family or those you trust; they will
help keep you on track. It is always more fun when
you celebrate your achievements with your loved
ones around you.

STEP III: *Take Action*

*"Go confidently in the direction of your dreams! Live
the life you've imagined."*—Henry David Thoreau

So I had the goals on the bathroom mirror, the plans written in
my bedside notebook, and my resources gathered. It was time to
stop writing, talking, and planning. It was time to take action. At
this point, I took a step that would commit me to my goal. I hired
a manager, or I hired movers, or I bought a nonrefundable ticket
to Paris. Each one of these actions made my goals feel more real
and thus increased my level of commitment. From there, I thought,
"Okay, you're really doing this. Keep going."

I'll be honest. It's not always easy when you are going after your
initial goals. For example, when I decided to go back to work, I was
still living in Miami, but most of my work was based in LA. If there
was an audition or a job, I had to get on a plane and fly across the
country. This is not easy when you have two toddlers. I could not
keep dragging them to the airport every time I got a call, but I did
not want to leave them for any length of time. I was leaving them
with my mother or Jinny, but I still couldn't bear to leave them for
more than a day. Most often, I would get on a plane in the morning, arrive in LA for the audition or job, and hop back on a plane as
soon as I was done. And while the whole process was absolutely exhausting, it was also exhilarating. For me, the key to keeping myself

going was to focus on the feeling of exhilaration rather than the exhaustion. As long as I felt proud and confident, as long as I let myself stop every once in a while to recognize that I was doing the right thing, I was happy and could keep moving forward.

When I did stop for the first time to look around at the outcome of my actions, I realized that I was a better mother, daughter, sister, and friend, because I felt I had my life back in my hands. Even though I was busy, I felt as though I was giving more to my sons, because I had achievements that I was proud of and a future to look forward to. I was not about to let go of any of that this time around.

Note from Jinny

ON TAKING ACTION

Although this may seem like the last step in making a change, it is in fact the beginning of a working process. It is not always easy, especially at the beginning when it is very hard to believe in results. Don't let this discourage you; keep moving forward because you are building confidence with every small step you make. Once you start to see results and celebrate your successes with your support system, you will be more inclined to work harder and harder to achieve your final goals. This process is going to also give you the opportunity to grow as an individual and find wonderful things about yourself that you wouldn't otherwise discover. This is a learning opportunity. Enjoy this process and allow yourself to be proud of what you have learned and the new skills you have acquired.

> When making changes, it is important to remember that it often takes three to six months to modify behaviors, so stick with it. Do not worry. It will become easier and eventually it will become second nature.

STEP IV: *Keep the Cycle Going*
"Many people have dreams. Very few do something to make them happen."—Jose I. Alvarez

For me, the beauty of reaching each new goal was that it made me want to set another. Now that the cycle was in motion, I did not want to stop it. My first goal (going back to work) bled into my second goal (moving to LA), and I began the process all over again. It was only three months from the moment I made the decision to when I made the move. For me, this was a no-brainer. Once I made the decision, I did not take the time to reconsider staying in Miami. I knew I had to leave. I had to start completely anew. I had to be on my own and rely on nobody but myself.

I hired movers, I started looking for an apartment, I began researching schools for the boys, and the hardest part of all, I broke it to my family and friends in Miami. It was extremely difficult to leave behind everyone in Miami. Jinny was there. Mom was there. Jose and his entire family were there. I had this incredible cocoon around me in Miami . . . and that is exactly why I had to leave. Unless I forced myself, I would never leave the cocoon and explore the world. And as warm, cozy and reassuring as it was to be in the cocoon, I simply had to go out and face the world by myself. Had I not done that, I would have never become the butterfly that I wanted to be.

And I was right. The minute I got to LA, I became a lot more independent. In Miami, I stuck to a routine: Take the boys to school, go to the gym, run errands, repeat. But in LA, I had a sense of adventure. During the two years I lived in Miami I didn't know how to get anywhere without my GPS, yet after a week in LA, I knew how to navigate the freeways GPS-free. And in a matter of weeks, I had more friends than I had made in the entire two years in Miami. The difference was, I wanted to own this city. I wanted to learn the freeways, the side streets, and all of the ins and outs. I wanted to establish a strong network and have a big group of friends to invite over for Sunday barbecues. I was intent on claiming LA as my own. It was my city. Nobody had chosen it for me; I chose it for myself. And that's what makes it all the more beautiful in my eyes.

I only recently realized that by being here, I have come full circle. I don't plan on leaving LA anytime soon. This is the place I was headed to all those years ago when I met my ex in the nightclub in Puerto Rico. Do I regret having met him then? Not at all. I would not be the strong, stable person I am today. I would not have had my boys, the loves of my life. I would not fully understand the importance of hanging on to my own dreams and going for them. Every day I am in Los Angeles reminds me to go after my dreams and to keep my cycle of Rediscovery in motion . . . and that is why I pursued my third goal only three months after I moved into my new California home. Although it was seemingly the "least important" of the three goals I had set out for myself in the beginning, it was crucial in teaching me a lesson about myself, and that is that I deserve to be happy!

I bought the plane ticket to Paris so that I could finally see the city the way I wanted to see it and get on a bicycle to go buy bread. Don't ask me what the bread thing is about. I'm not sure. I guess it has just always been my image of Paris: a girl on a bike going to buy bread (or that is always where I imagine the Parisian girls are riding off to). I had been in Paris a few times before, but I had never seen anything but the insides of hotel rooms or town cars. This time, I was going to see every part of that city. My friend Omar knew every little nook that we had to go to—every great little café, every big tourist trap, every little crepe stand—so my planning consisted of buying the plane tickets and depending on Omar to be my guide!

Once we touched down in Paris, we started to take the town by storm. Or at least the crepe stands. I made it a rule that I had to have at least one crepe with Nutella per day, sometimes two. We went to the Eiffel Tower and Montmartre; we spent hours people watching at the little cafés; and of course, we rode our bikes to get bread. I cannot tell you how free and content I felt at that moment. As I coasted along the Parisian streets, I suddenly realized how far I had come and how much farther I would go—my ride was just beginning.

The first time I went to Paris, I went with a friend, and I fell in love with the city. I remember thinking how much I wanted my boys to see the magic of the place, so I organized a trip for the following New Year's. I went with my boys and some of my best friends and their families. We spent a week walking along the same streets and saw the New Year's fireworks near the Eiffel Tower. That is when I realized the truth to the saying that Paris is the most romantic city in the world, and I thought how great it would be there with a man I loved.

A few months ago my boyfriend surprised me by taking me to my favorite city, and I got to be the tour guide. We didn't ride bikes that time. Instead we went out in a rowboat on the Seine. He rowed as I ate a baguette and ruminated on the fact that I had been in Paris so many times during my marriage and never once did I think to do this. Never once did I even see the Eiffel Tower, but now I cannot see going to Paris without that tower, those baguettes, and those crepes. It's almost embarrassing for me to say that all the times I had been in the city before my trip with Omar, my knowledge of Paris was restricted to the inside of hotels, radio stations, and TV studios. Of course, I could have gone out to see the city, but I knew that everyone else was working or resting for work, so I just went along with it. I don't think I ever realized the lunacy of it all. Who goes to Paris and doesn't see the Eiffel Tower! Well, not me. Not anymore. That day in Paris on the Seine with my boyfriend, I took the time to look back and see how much I had changed since my divorce. I had allowed myself to change, and used my divorce as the catalyst. I felt so very proud of myself. It felt amazing to sit back for a moment, let someone else row for a little bit, and just let myself feel proud. You will have this moment too, and when you do, remember to take it in, savor it, and cherish it. You've earned it!

With every new goal I achieved, I started to add more goals to my list to fill in the holes. I am constantly reassessing that list, seeing if I still want to go after all of those goals, and even reprioritizing it. Certain goals that seemed absolutely dire a few years ago are perhaps not so important anymore and vice versa. My needs and desires are constantly changing, and that is exactly what this Rediscovery cycle is all about: change. What's most important is that I remain in control of the decisions I make, and that I always remain true to myself as I live the life I have carved out for myself.

Note from Jinny

ON KEEPING THE CYCLE GOING

In this stage, you are definitely breathing freely. You have been able to take control of your life again. You have been able to identify your dreams, create an action plan, work toward your goals, and most important, make changes. This is a process that you haven't been able to accomplish right after divorce. But now you are more than capable of keeping all these achievements going. Keeping the cycle going is not the end of your process; it only represents the beginning of the new you, the life that you have back in your own hands. And now you can focus on working on new goals.

The Tools

Helping Yourself in
Your Rediscovery

"I never lose sight of the
fact that just being is fun."
—Katharine Hepburn

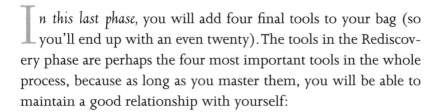

I n *this last phase,* you will add four final tools to your bag (so you'll end up with an even twenty). The tools in the Rediscovery phase are perhaps the four most important tools in the whole process, because as long as you master them, you will be able to maintain a good relationship with yourself:

1. Recognize your new priorities.
2. Find your own answers.
3. Discover new passions.
4. Find healthy new relationships.

1. *Recognize your priorities*

"Once you figure out who you are
and what you love about yourself, I think it all
kinda falls into place."—Jennifer Aniston

In one of my many notebooks, there is a "Priority Chart" that I recently drafted:

Priorities Before Marriage	Priorities During Marriage	Priorities After Marriage
1. My Career	1. Relationship	1. Motherhood
2. My Family	2. Motherhood	2. Myself
3. Myself	3. My Family	3. Career
4. Romantic Relationships		4. My Family
5. My Friends		5. Romantic Relationship
		6. Friends

After I looked at this chart, it was a shocking realization that I had let three important priorities (myself, my career, and my friends) fall so completely out of the box during my marriage. Today I have six priorities, which I strive on a daily basis to keep in order. My decision-making process is much easier because of this chart, which is planted somewhere in my mind. For example, my children are my number-one priority, so every decision I make, I make with my boys in mind.

I was on a talk show recently, and I stated my priorities clearly. To paraphrase: "I am a single mom and it is very difficult. I want to have a balance between being a mom and having a career. My most important role is being a mom. Whatever comes after is secondary. I try to balance my roles as much as possible. The time that I am not with the boys, when they are in school, is when I can focus on my stuff, go on auditions, go to the gym, etcetera. But when I pick them up from school at four, it is all about them. No phones, no Internet. It is difficult, but not impossible. My intent is to be present when I am with my kids and to really be there. I don't want them to grow up and say, "My mom was never there." I want them to say, "My mom was there for us. She was strong. She kept moving forward, she kept working, and she was happy." Because I have my priorities in order, I constantly have this mentality in mind. Therefore, every goal I set and every plan I make stem from this belief.

Note from Jinny

ON RECOGNIZING YOUR PRIORITIES

Once you figure out your top priorities, remind yourself of them on a daily basis. Obviously, you have to be honest when you assess these priorities. Do not worry that you are going to be hurting anyone's feelings by placing them below your career, for example. If that is the way you need to organize your priorities at this point in your life, do not make any apologies for it. As soon as you have your priorities in order, everything will fall into place.

2. *Find Your Own Answers*

"It is well that the earth is round that we do not
see too far ahead."—Meryl Streep

At times, this is the best part about being single again. Everything is up to you to decide! I suppose you can perceive it as lonely and depressing to always be the one deciding. But you can also view it as an empowering and exhilarating opportunity. I chose to go the "empowering and exhilarating" route. I highly recommend it. I was excited when I chose our new house. I chose the new neighborhood we were going to live in. I chose the schools the boys were going to go, etc. I'd like to give you a formula for how to find your own answers, but sometimes it feels as though I am just making it up as I go along. I guess because I am! I am a big believer in gut feelings, but I am also a big believer in plans. When I am searching for my own answers, I tend to decide half on gut instinct and half on planning (it sounds contradictory, but it works somehow for me). You have to find the method that works for you and that you are comfortable pursuing. A lot about this new phase and finding your own answers will be based on pure trial and error. None of us is going to have all the answers. We are not God. The best way I know how to proceed is to:

1. Make a plan
2. Trust my gut instinct
3. Be willing to stumble

Note from Jinny

ON FINDING YOUR OWN ANSWERS

Don't be so hard on yourself; you don't have to have all the answers right away. Understand that you may never have all of the answers. That's why God created friends, family, and therapists. This is the time to think about yourself, think about what you have accomplished, and plan for what you want to become. This is a new and exciting chapter in your life, and it is up to you to write it. It's not easy, but you need to find the way to take control of your thoughts, behavior, and life. Invest all of your energy in this new change that life is giving you.

3. *Discover New Passions*

"So much to do, so little done, such things to be."—Elizabeth Taylor

Ah, the fun part. I had a whole list of new passions that I jumped into headlong. It has since been pared down, but I do recommend that you explore any passion that you desire. Later on, you can decide which hobbies you want to pursue further, but at the beginning of your Rediscovery, go ahead and try them all! Some of passions I set out to try were flamenco dancing, traveling for pleasure, reading for pleasure, gardening, writing, photography, and drawing and designing clothes. Of course there are more, and I am still pursuing some of these passions. Others I have decided were not for me. But the best move I made was never saying no to any of my inner voices saying, "Let's learn to flamenco!" or "Let's redo the front garden!" I still carry this attitude with me when it comes to discovering new passions. I never thought I was going to adore flamenco as much as I do, but I am so glad that I accepted the challenge!

4. *Find Healthy New Relationships*

"The best thing to hold on to in life is each other."—Audrey Hepburn

When I was ready for a serious relationship I was *really* ready. I knew that it would not be fair to myself or anyone else if I rushed into a relationship right after my marriage; I just was not ready. I waited until I was in a happy, healthy place and I had unloaded the baggage from my past relationship. When I finally began to go out on dates, I almost felt bad for the guys. I had my guard up because I did not want to make the same mistakes that I had in my marriage. But also, I had my children to think about, and I did not want to let anyone into their lives, or into my house for that matter, until I was sure that the relationship was solid and stable. For the first few years, when the doorbell would ring for a date, I would sprint down the stairs from my bedroom, kiss the boys goodbye, and then slip out the door without letting my date set foot in the house. I remember one guy asking me after the fourth or fifth time I slipped through the front door, "Do you think I can go inside the house one day?" Poor guy. But he never did make it in—he didn't meet the rigorous screening system I had set in place, which was pretty simple: If he was not good enough for my boys, he was not good enough for me. The screening system helped me to weed out the not-so-good dates much more easily, and it took me (or us) four years until I (or we) found a man who passed the test. Still, my boyfriend was introduced to Cristian and Ryan as my friend, and for the first five or six months, my boys regarded him as my friend. It was actually my sons who wanted him to be my boyfriend. Their father had remarried, and in their minds, it was only natural for me to have someone too. They kept saying, "He should be your boyfriend." And it was only then, after my boys had given their outright approval and my boyfriend and I were secure in our relationship, that I told Cristian and Ryan that he was more than a friend.

Just like LA came full circle, love did too. I do not know what the future holds for me, but I have to say that today I'm living an incredible chapter in my life. I am letting myself be loved for once; I have allowed myself to let go of so many fears and just fall in love. This incredible man loves me completely and, what's more, he adores my boys. Every plan is made with my boys in mind. He gets home and they run, screaming his name and jumping all over him. He brings them so much joy and he has his own place in our hearts. They admire him, respect him and in their own little way thank him for the happiness he brings. He supports me in every way and is proud of every milestone I achieve. In so many ways, he forces me to be better. But most of all his greatest gift has been to let me know that it is possible to find someone to love me, and that it makes no difference to him that I have kids and that they are before him. My biggest fear was that I would never find a man like this. I feared that nobody would be able to love me so completely. I feared that it was not possible to find someone who accepted every aspect of who I was, where I had been, and where I was going. And then I met this incredible man who taught me to let go of all the fear, hold on to my dreams and just love and be loved purely, simply and completely.

I believe Audrey Hepburn said it best (didn't she always?), when she said, "Your heart just breaks, that's all. But you can't judge, or point fingers. You just have to be lucky enough to find someone who appreciates you." Yes, the heart "just breaks," and it may break again, but you will be okay. No matter what may happen, there will always be someone out there who will love and appreciate you for who you are. To settle for anything less is to cheat yourself of the kind of relationship you deserve. Looking back, I can say that the greatest gift was the time I spent learning to love and appreciate myself first. Once you can learn to do this, you will be capable of letting someone love and appreciate the strong, stable woman you have become.

Note from Jinny

ON FINDING HEALTHY NEW RELATIONSHIPS

In order for you to find healthy new relationships, it is crucial for you to take as long as you need to compose yourself and to put all the pieces of the puzzle together. Take into consideration that this might take some time. Rushing into a relationship before you are ready is not fair to anyone, least of all you. You have to comprehend and fully digest what went wrong in your marriage, in order to "empty your bag." Make a fresh new start and take the past as a learning experience.

~~~~~~

Final Words on Rediscovery

"Pick the day. Enjoy it—to the hilt. The day as it comes. People as they come... The past, I think, has helped me appreciate the present—and I don't want to spoil any of it by fretting about the future."—Audrey Hepburn

Some mornings I get up and it seems as though I am unstoppable. I have that watch-out-here-I-come attitude, and I take full advantage of it. I hit the ground running, and I go all day. I'll go for a workout, work for a few hours, start redecorating plans for a room in the house, and pick up the boys from school and take them to the park or the batting cages. Then we'll come home to do homework, and I'll cook dinner. Then it's bathtime and bedtime. When I lie down at night, I am amazed at all that I can do in one day and so proud of myself for getting to this place.

And then there are mornings when I wake up and already feel tired. On those days, I shower, get the boys off to school, and then do something that I know will make me feel happy, energized, and productive. I'll do whatever I have to do to get myself going. And I always remind myself that these days of downtime are part of life. You can't go on four cylinders every day; your engine is going to give out on you completely. So sometimes I'll just sit down and watch *Breakfast at Tiffany's* at ten in the morning. Because I can. Because it makes me happy. Because some days I need to watch Holly Golightly commiserate with me about having the "the mean reds," which are of course worse than the blues. "The mean reds are horrible," Holly says. "Suddenly you're afraid and you don't know what you're afraid of. Do you ever get that feeling?" And I will pretend she is talking to me and say, "Yes! I have them today!" And Holly will tell me, "The only thing that does any good is to jump in a cab and go to Tiffany's."

131

I've learned that "jumping in a cab and going to Tiffany's" can take on many different forms. It can mean pumping up the music and having a dance session with my boys. Or going to the gym for a spinning class. Or calling a friend to meet for coffee and good conversation. Maybe I will sit down and write for a few hours. Or maybe I'll call my dad or my brothers, who I know can always make me laugh. Or I'll plan an extra family outing or a craft for the boys and me to do together. I'll go to the teacher supply store and get excited about making a macramé dinosaur! I'll do whatever it takes to get myself out of "the mean reds." I have yet to literally jump in the cab and go to Tiffany's, but perhaps the next time I'm in New York, I'll give it a shot. Until then, I am doing just fine with my DVD and my metaphorical methods.

I want to continually learn about myself and challenge myself. I want to feel unstoppable some days and inexplicably tired the next, because this means that I am finally challenging myself again. I am finally having a real and healthy relationship with me. I am discovering the Yari that I always wanted to be. And you know what I'm finding out? She's pretty damn cool.

Part Four

Commonly Asked Questions

"Life works out—but not
as you expect it."
—*French Proverb*

THE QUESTIONS DURING THE ACCEPTANCE PHASE

I had *so many* questions when I was working through this first phase (and all the phases for that matter). Honestly, I didn't want to ask anyone for help, advice, or answers. First of all, I did not have the energy to engage in long conversations about these issues. I just wanted short, concise answers, but we all know that once you start asking someone questions, the conversation can get much deeper and much longer than you anticipated. And that's not always what you're in the mood for when you're mourning a divorce. I know that I would have liked to have my questions asked and answered in book form so that I could control how long the conversation would last and I could continually refer to the answers. I spoke to my friends, and we have compiled a list of the most common questions that we had during this phase. Jinny and I have tried to answer in the most concise manner possible. I have taken my experience out of the equation, and we have responded so that these answers can serve to help you no matter what the details of your particular divorce experience may be.

How do I let others help me during this Acceptance phase?

People can help you, but you have to help yourself first. This means that you must know who your friends really are and trust your instincts. Be aware of how you feel when you are around certain people, and you will be able to decide who will be able to support you and who will only promote negative energy. During the Rebuilding phase, it is critical that you surround yourself with people who will not throw more fuel onto the fire. You are sweating enough, mind you. You need to surround yourself with positive friends and family, who will promote an encouraging attitude and optimistic outlook.

There are many factors that you cannot control during your divorce, but one thing you are fully in charge of is the company you keep. Remember that if you are surrounded with positive individuals, you will start thinking positively, acting in a positive way, and interacting with others in a positive manner. This will create a cycle of positive energy that it is hard for others to break.

Conversely, if you are surrounded with negative individuals—individuals who will join you in criticizing, hating, or gossiping about your ex—you will be apt to think and act in a negative way. This too creates a cycle that is hard to break, and it is a destructive and damaging cycle. You can get stuck in this negative cycle and continue to surround yourself with individuals who will constantly berate your ex-spouse and throw fuel onto the fire for as long as you let them. At first, it may feel good to warm yourself by this fire. Why not just sit around and listen to others tell you how horrible the situation is? First, it will not get you any closer to recovery. Second, it will be that much harder to break this negativity. And third, for every day you spend engaging in negativity, you are losing a day you could have used positively. Remember that the optimism with which you tackle this stage will directly affect the way you rebuild and regain control over your life.

Be smart! Follow your instincts and only invite people into your life who can actually help you in your recovery. Ask the others to come back later.

How do I explain the divorce to the kids?

Before you even attempt to break it to your children, you have to know, and truly believe, that you have made the right decision for them and for you. Often we think that we should stay with our partners for the sake of our children. What we fail to realize is that raising children in an unhealthy home environment is, in fact, far more traumatizing than raising a child in a divorced, tension-free household. When you are ready to tell your children, keep in mind:

1. No matter the age of your children, you must tell them about the divorce. Explain it to each child on a level that they can understand.
2. If one parent has played a stronger parenting role, that parent should break the news to the child so as to lessen the trauma.
3. It is important that no blame be assigned to either parent for the separation and/or divorce. This may give the child a reason to choose sides, and it is unhealthy to have a good-versus-bad-parent dynamic.
4. Make sure the children know that they are not the reason for the divorce. A child's first reaction is to think that it is his/her

own fault. Stress the fact that the divorce is between the parents and not the children. If they have this clear, they will better understand that they cannot be responsible for the reconciliation.

5. Do not break the news unless the divorce is definitely going to take place. For example, if it is a trial separation, do not use the word "divorce."

6. Break the news when you can be together for a long period of time, e.g., the weekend. Children need your support and your presence so that they can feel safe and secure.

7. After breaking the news, give the children some idea of what they should expect in the future, especially when living arrangements, school arrangements, etc. are about to change.

8. Know that when children ask, "Why?" they are not asking for details about the breakup of your marriage. They are asking, "Why is this happening to me?" Therefore what your children need is for you to reaffirm that you and your spouse still love them just the same and you will be better parents if you are not married, but just friends.

9. Always leave the door open for your children to ask questions. It is important for them to understand that they can trust you and that they can find a friend in you. It is also important to remain truthful, patient (no matter how hard this is), and supportive.

What issues should I be prepared for after I tell my children?

1. When children find out that their parents are getting a divorce, they often feel anger and humiliation. There are common reactions, because the children are losing their old family structure.

2. Children will feel that nobody understands what they are going through.

3. They may withdraw and lose interest in hobbies, school, friends, and the general enjoyment of life.

4. Children are very intuitive; they have probably sensed for a long time that things weren't right between Mom and Dad.

5. Don't be surprised if the children seem to take their anger out on you, or lay a guilt trip on you about the divorce. You are the person who is most available, and with whom they feel safe expressing their emotions. This is a natural and normal part of their grieving process.

How do I help my children work through these issues?

1. Provide a stable environment by implementing a regular household schedule, and clear rules and regulations.

2. Offer your continuing encouragement.

3. Do NOT lean on your children for emotional support, but let them lean on you. Never make them feel like your happiness depends on them.

4. Let them know that they count and that you will always be there to listen to their problems.

5. Let them know that it is OKAY to love both parents and that they will always be loved enormously by both of you.

How do I maintain a healthy relationship with my ex?

It is important to recognize that you can end the conflict, heal the hurt, and restore love, not necessarily as husband and wife, but as one human being to another. The key to healing your relationship is you. How you act toward your ex largely determines how he will act toward you. You decide whether the relationship is painful or supportive. To have a relationship work, you need to learn to love each other as ex-husband and ex-wife. It's a different relationship from the one you used to have, but an important one nonetheless. You can create this love by giving the gift of acceptance and appreciation. When you feel great, you feel better about yourself and better about your life, and you also feel better about the person who accepts and appreciates you.

How do I keep my children's father in their lives?

As hard as this might be, it is so important to keep your children's father in their lives. I know it might sound impossible, especially if the reasons for your divorce were very painful, but the truth of the matter is that the divorce is between you two. He will always be their father. Whether he wants to be part of their lives or not, we, as mothers, carry the responsibility to raise our children to be as healthy and happy as possible. I know I have said I don't want my boys to grow up and have any issues, so every day when, out of nowhere, they ask for him, I will always say he is extremely busy working. I will assure them that he will come pick them up very soon. I will let them know that he's always thinking about them, and how much he misses them and loves them.

I know in situations some fathers want nothing to do with their children. They leave and never even care to ask about the kids. If the kids are old enough to understand this situation (i.e., fully grown), it is easier to be honest and let them know the truth. But, if the kids are too young to understand, be the stronger one and cover up for now. Don't ever talk negatively in front of the kids and make sure that your friends know that this is your rule. Not everybody has kids, so they are not aware that children listen to everything we say even when they seem distracted watching a movie. Once you are a mother, your entire vision and mission in life changes completely. For instance, you don't rush through a yellow light; you are constantly checking expiration dates; you make sure the house is child-proof. We have to be just as cautious about preserving our children's relationships with their fathers.

If it is possible, put your pride aside and be the one to make the phone calls to keep your children and their father connected. There are times that you may have to plan ahead by making sure to buy an extra birthday or Christmas gift and put his name on it. Be the one to choose a day and time of the week when the kids can talk to him. Sometimes it's all a matter of communication to somehow make fathers aware of how much the kids miss him. Many times their own guilt and embarrassment make them stay away from their kids.

In my situation, my sons' father exists in their everyday lives, especially in their own environment. My boys' rooms are filled with pictures of their father and them together. (If you do not have these pictures, ask your children's father to take pictures of them together next time he has them for a weekend.) Every night we pray for him, and we talk about him often. All of these seemingly small acts can and will make a huge difference for your child, which should always be our first priority as mothers.

How do I react when my ex is not "playing fair"?

Do not forget that a good relationship depends on the attitudes of two people. You cannot control your ex-spouse's attitude, but you can control your own attitude, and this will most certainly affect

how your ex-spouse reacts to you. If you are pleasant and positive, it is much harder for him to be angry and rude back. If at
first your ex-husband does react with anger and bitterness, do
not come down to his level. Maintain an aura of maturity. This can
be incredibly difficult to do, but if you have to, just remind yourself that by staying mature you are staying in control of the situation. Eventually, he will strive to come up to your level.

One thing you can do is make a list of some of the wonderful
things that your ex-husband has brought into your life. This can
be hard at the beginning, so you can even include the little
things, if you cannot credit him with big contributions. But eventually, you will probably recognize that your ex-husband gave
you many gifts that it is hard to credit him with in the throes of a
divorce. You may be grasping at straws by the end, but that's okay.
Write down some of the "gifts," no matter how minor they may
seem. Here are some examples:

He gave you your children!
He made you laugh.
He brought out the kid in you.
He introduced you to great friends.
He taught you how to stick up for yourself.

Writing out a list like this will inspire you to act gracefully and
in turn inspire him. What's most important is that you remain
true to yourself, the smart and intelligent person who you are, no
matter how "dirty" or how "unfair" he may be playing.

How do I overcome the feeling of failure?

In order to overcome this feeling, you have to understand it. You
will experience this feeling, because when you get married you

felt that you accomplished a major and very important milestone in your life. Knocking down that milestone can give you a feeling of failure; however, you need to understand that you are getting a divorce because you were not in a healthy relationship anymore, and being in an unhealthy relationship will prevent you from accomplishing other great feats. Getting married should not be your final milestone in life. Ideally, if you are in a healthy marriage, you can reach goals and conquer wonderful feats with your partner's support and encouragement. However, if you are not in such a relationship, it is up to you to be strong enough to realize this. This is a difficult task, but if you do come to this realization and make the decision to separate from your partner because the marriage is not working, that is an accomplishment in and of itself. Think about this realization as a new milestone; you have been healthy and strong enough to recognize the reality of your marriage and to make a move in the right direction. So do not feel as though you have failed. Failure would have been to stay in a marriage that does not make both of you better, healthier, and happier people every day.

Does everyone go through the feeling of failure? Is it possible not to?

Yes, everyone goes through this feeling. As with every decision we make in life, we may question ourselves and wonder, "Am I doing the right thing? Am I doing the best thing for myself, my future, my children?" Socially, we have been predisposed to believe that "marriage is for life." After all, you do say "till death do us part," and it is written in the Bible, but as a priest and good friend once told us, "I do not think God wants to see you live out your days miserably." We are sure that God wants us to be happy and needs us to be 100 percent of the people we are capable of; how can you be 100 percent of yourself if you are in a toxic relationship? Marriage should be for life if you are happy in your relationship and if you are truly a better person when you are with your partner. Do not be so hard on yourself if it didn't work out; be sad, but also be proud of yourself for recognizing that you will be a better person if you and your partner separate. Your family, your friends, and your community will benefit if you allow yourself to once again be 100 percent of yourself.

When should I stop crying?

When you are ready! When we cry, it is because we are experiencing feelings and emotions that our body cannot deal with or control. When you allow yourself to cry, you are acknowledging that there is something heavy that you need to deal with; you are recognizing that this situation is hard and it hurts, but you are being realistic about it. After you cry, physically, your body will feel a sense of relief. You will feel emotionally lighter, because you have let your emotions out into the air and you are now ready to recharge.

Every time you don't allow yourself to cry, you may feel that you are being strong and stoic; however, there is only so much that your body can handle. If you keep bottling up your emotions, you will eventually have a breakdown when you cannot handle it anymore.

Why should we let ourselves grieve the loss of a relationship?

Going through the grieving process is a natural and necessary aspect of recovery and rediscovery. When you allow yourself to grieve the loss of a relationship, you are allowing yourself to experience the pain until the wound is completely healed. When you don't allow yourself time to go through this process, you are leaving that wound open and it will never fully close until you give yourself permission to grieve. You can cover up the gore with a good-looking bandage, but underneath the bandage, the gore is still there. You have to let it breathe!

How do I let myself grieve without getting stuck?

Understand that you should cry when you need to cry and allow yourself to have bad days because of the loss. That said, you should recognize that the grieving process is exactly that: a process that needs to have an end. You are grieving not so that you can stay stuck in the past, but so you can be healthy enough to move into the future. Remember that you are creating your own future with each thought, word, and act; even on the days when you feel paralyzed by grief, do something good for yourself. Tell yourself something reassuring and positive, no matter how insignificant it may seem.

How do I tell my family and friends?

Some people include their family and friends in the discussion from day one. Others don't tell their family and friends until they know it is over. I know that I told my family members from the very beginning because I knew that I could not get through this without them; however, I did not tell all of my friends right away because I wasn't ready. It is important to be in a healthy place before you tell most people about your decision. You cannot control how they are going to react to your telling them about the divorce; you can only control how YOU react, so prepare yourself. For me, the best way to break the news was to say, "My husband and I have decided to divorce. It wasn't working out." Remember: You don't owe anyone a further explanation. I know how easy it is to fall into the trap of answering question after question, such as:

Are you sure?
Is there nothing else you can do?
How long has this been going on?
Who made the decision?
What happened?

The questions are endless, but know that you do not have to answer them. You do not owe anybody any further answers. In fact, you owe it to yourself not to answer. First of all, responding to these questions is not going to help you in your recovery. Second of all, once you open yourself up and start entertaining these questions, a line has been crossed, and these friends and family members will continue with their "helpful" interrogations. Set the stage early on for how you want people to act toward you, so when they start inquiring, all you have to say is "I am not ready to talk about it. Let's talk about something else!" Eventually (hopefully immediately) the questions will stop.

How do I become stable enough?

You feel as if you have been thrown into a dark hole, and you will never be able to climb out and get back on steady ground. At first, you barely have the strength to stand up, let alone climb. But the great part of life is that you will get thrown ropes when you least expect them. The key is you have to be smart enough to take them. For example, when my son came in and told me, "Everything is going to be fine!" I decided to take hold of that "rope" and begin the climb. I could have continued crying. It would have been easy enough to scoop him up in my arms and continue crying, but that would not have been fair to either of us.

Your children can tell when you are unsteady even when you are not crying. They feel the instability and will mimic you. When you are flopping about, this is the most damaging time for your children. Once Mommy is okay, the kids will be okay. Realizing this was the first rope for me and from then on, I grabbed on to every little thread that would help me in my climb.

Am I strong enough?

Believe me, I asked myself this question often. I remember telling Jinny that I didn't think I was and I remember her answer:

> What kind of question is that? Look at how strong you have been already. It is easy and safe to hold out hope that everything will work out, but it takes a strong, brave person to realize that she has to make a decision. You have done this already and making that decision was the strongest, bravest action you could have taken.

I did not consider my decision a strong action at first, but Jinny's words helped me to see that it was. From this knowledge, I began to find strength where I thought there was none. I started to believe in myself and what I could accomplish.

THE QUESTIONS IN THE REBUILDING PHASE

The Rebuilding phase is more about asking questions of yourself and less about seeking answers from others. You have to get your life in order and you have to do it on your own terms. I found that many of the questions I asked when I was rebuilding were questions that nobody but me could answer; however, there are a few questions that Jinny and I came up with that we thought would be helpful to have someone else answer as well. Above all, remember that you have to find your own answers to your questions.

What are the first elements of my life that I should put in order?

The first element you need to put in order is you. The most important person in this Rebuilding phase is you and only you. Even though you may not be used to putting yourself first, this is the one time in your life that you have to be a little selfish. You are only being selfish today so that one day you can be the person that your children, family, and friends deserve to have. What do they tell you to do on an airplane "in the event of an emergency"? You have to put the oxygen mask on yourself first so that you are stable enough to help those around you. You need to help yourself before you can help anyone else. This is a crucial point to understand, especially if you have children. Children, friends, and family will react to the "emergency situations" based on how you are acting. If you are calm and dealing with the situation in a healthy manner, everyone around you will follow suit. If you take the time to focus on yourself, you will be able to deal with any situation calmly, and then, and only then, will you be a positive aid to your children, family, and friends.

How do I get my balance back?

When we experience new and challenging changes in our life, our balance seems to shake. Don't worry. It is completely normal and you need to let it happen. You can work toward getting that balance back by identifying your priorities. When you identify these priorities, you will realize that things that were once so important are not important at all anymore. You will need to stop and think. Organize your life and do not only identify your priorities, but identify the steps you are going to take to establish a healthy and exciting balance in your life. Take one step at a time. Think about one priority, and don't worry about how you are going to tackle the others. They will fall into place as you go. You cannot fix your life in a single day. Take your time.

Steps for establishing a healthy and exciting balance in your life:

1. **Identify your roles:** In this step, you are to identify the many roles you possess in life. Examples: **A mother, a professional, a sister, a daughter, a friend, and many more.**

2. **Prioritize your roles:** Once you have identified your roles, it is time to prioritize them. In this step, honesty is the most important element. This is very personal and you are not to judge yourself. Be realistic and be true to yourself, as long as you do not jeopardize the well-being of others. Example:

    1. A mother
    2. A professional
    3. A friend
    4. A daughter
    5. A sister

Identify potential areas of improvement in each of these roles. EXAMPLE: *As a mother, I vow to spend more quality time with my children.*

3. **Make a plan:** You need a plan to support the areas of improvement in each role and help you to keep your intentions in check. *Example:* Instead of focusing on taking the children on grand outings, I will focus on maintaining their day-to-day activities. The grand trips or over-the-top gestures are not the norm and last for only a short period of time; however, simple and day-to-day activities such as trip to the grocery store, a bike ride, doing homework together, or watching a video are much easier for me to achieve. It will also reassure the children that everything in their lives has changed for the better.

4. **Take action:** The last but most important step in achieving a balance is taking action. Here is when you start taking control and changing your life. **Implement the plan you have created.**

How do I know when I'm ready to move on (or have already moved on to) the Rebuilding phase?

There is not a specific time or space that will guide you in the process. Moving from the Acceptance phase into the Rebuilding phase entails accepting the reality, dropping the hope that everything can be worked out, and then taking control of your life. This represents the biggest transition in the process. You are only ready to move from one phase to the next when you have emptied your bag completely. Imagine yourself going to a market with no concrete floor; the floor is full of sand and rocks. You enter the market with the shopping cart and start adding items. The more items you add, the heavier the shopping cart gets. At one point you will realize that no matter how hard you push the shopping cart, it will not move. At that time, you have to start taking items from the cart. Remove as much of the denial, guilt, anger, and pain as possible. You will not unload it all just yet, and that is okay. But you are ready to move from the Acceptance phase into the Rebuilding phase when the shopping cart is light enough to move.

How can I focus only on myself when I have children to look after and care for? Shouldn't they be the priority?

Focusing on yourself only does not mean that you need to be locked in a room and detached from the real world. You cannot stop time. Life continues. Acceptance, Rebuilding, and Rediscovery are inner phases you need to go through in order to take control over your life. Your children are definitely important in your life and you want to be the best and do the best for them. In order for you to do that, you need to focus on yourself first. You need to be emotionally, mentally, and physically healthy in order to be the best of what you can be as a mother. You need to be happy in order for them to be happy. As a matter of fact, children are a powerful source of energy and strength; they can definitely help you along the way by simply bringing their pure laughter and unconditional love into your life.

I am constantly afraid of failing every time I make a decision. What can I do to free myself from this fear?

Experiencing fear of failure is completely normal after a divorce, especially when the immediate reaction is "I made a mistake." First, you need to understand that getting married was not a mistake; just because you are getting a divorce does not mean that you made a bad decision. Actually, getting a divorce when the relationship is not working is, in fact, a good decision. It would not be fair for you to stay in a relationship that was not fulfilling your needs and giving you happiness.

Second, understand that fear is a feeling that you cannot change from one day to the next. However, you can decrease and even make the fear disappear with time and experience. The only thing you can do to free yourself from the fear of failing is taking control of your life, making decisions on your own, and allowing yourself to be successful. Internalizing that success is not measured by the result but by the process and experience you had to go through in order to find your happiness and get to where you are at the present time.

Does the Rebuilding phase move faster or slower than the Acceptance phase?

The speed and intensity with which you move through the phases varies from person to person. That said, in many cases the Rebuilding phase will go faster. This is because in the Acceptance phase, you have successfully dealt with the emotional and psychological stages and you are ready and eager to move on; however, if you find yourself stalling in this Rebuilding period, do not worry and never rush yourself. This is your divorce, and you must move through it at your own speed. Remember, the Rebuilding phase is about reconnecting with yourself.

How is the Acceptance phase different from the Rebuilding phase?

In the Acceptance phase, you are basically dealing with the situation, and your main focus is on the situation. You are struggling to understand what happened and struggling to recognize that perhaps the love of your life was not meant to be your life partner. In the Rebuilding phase, the main focus is on YOU. This phase marks the beginning of how your life is going to go forward. You have to set up the patterns and traditions for how you want your life to be from now on.

COMMONLY ASKED QUESTIONS DURING THE REDISCOVERY PERIOD

The commonly asked questions during the Rediscovery period tended to require either a very personal answer or a very professional answer. We decided to split the questions in half so that the personal questions are answered by Dayanara and the more professional questions are answered by Jinny.

From Me

How do you maintain the traditions and sense of family pride as a single parent?

I'm Puerto Rican, and though my boys were born in New York, they are both still Puerto Ricans. My parents did a great job of raising my brothers, my sister, and myself; they instilled a strong sense of family and a strong pride in our culture. Family is so important to me and keeping our traditions is a must:

1. Bendición! As soon as we see older relatives or speak to them on the phone, we ask for their blessing by saying: "Bendición!" He or she will respond, "Dios te bendiga." We perform this blessing ritual before we even say hello, and then we repeat the ritual when we say goodbye.
2. Every time we pass by a church, in our car or walking, we make the sign of the cross. My oldest son, Cristian, now stares at me to make sure I am doing it.
3. We attend church every Sunday.
4. Nightly prayers: Both boys say a prayer thanking God for all of their blessings and the prayer ends: "Thank you, God, for my

mom, my brother, and my family. Thank you for my dad and my dad's family. Thank you for what I am and what I have."

5. Three Kings' Day: In Puerto Rico, January 6 is just as important as December 24 and 25. The story goes that the three kings followed the star to get to baby Jesus and give him gifts. For the day before Three Kings' Day, we get shoe boxes and fill them will grass for the camels to eat. We place them under our beds, and in the morning, the grass will be gone and presents will be there!

6. Christmas: It has been a tradition for my family that no matter what, we will all be together on Christmas. My family from Puerto Rico comes to my house, and it is truly my favorite time of the year.

7. New Year's: We all go to Puerto Rico to bring in the New Year together. We basically eat, drink, and dance until we can't move anymore. We are from Puerto Rico—what do you expect?

8. Spanish: It is up to me that my boys keep our language. They were born and live in the United States, but it is very important to me that they learn and continue to speak Spanish as well as English.

9. Music: I am very conscious that the boys learn about Puerto Rican music. I was so excited the first time I saw that Cristian had rhythm. It was such a relief! Then it just happened with Ryan. I was really worried—it's no joke. I don't ever remember teaching them a step, but now that they are seven and four, I'm proud to say they already have some pretty great salsa steps down.

What are the benefits of parenting alone?

My favorite part of parenting alone is setting all of my own rules and on my own terms. Many of my rules and routines have come through trial and error. Babies do not come with a manual when they are born. I remember being at the hospital after having my first son. The morning after he was born, I fed him, and then the nurse came in to show me how to hold the baby for a bath. And that was it! Then she told me it was time to go home. I felt like everything was moving in fast-forward, and I said, "Wait! What do you mean I'm going home? What about everything else?" I wanted instructions. What happens during the day? What do I do when he coughs or doesn't want to eat? And, I actually did ask, "How do I know if all of his internal organs are working?" I am sure the nurse was laughing about that as she kicked me out of the hospital doors.

Since that day, I have gone about writing my own instruction manual, which is in a constant state of revision. After the divorce, the manual got a big overhaul. One of the greatest things I've noticed about being a single mom with two boys is that I can teach them how to be as polite as possible. I am preparing them to be perfect gentlemen. They know to be gentle and respect girls. They have been taught to treat girls as precious. As a game, we started our own "gentlemen rules." I would give Cristian scenarios for him to apply those rules. For instance:

RULE # 1—LADIES FIRST!
Scenario: "If you walk into a bus where there is one seat available, and it's only you and a girl standing . . . who gets it?"

RULE # 2—GENTLEMEN ALWAYS HELP OUT!
Scenario: "If you are in school and you see your friend struggling with her book bag, what do you offer?"
Scenario: "If you and your friend are walking toward the classroom and the door is closed, who should open the door?"

Scenario: "If you are at a friend's house and you are very thirsty, how do you ask for something to drink?"

I know that the day they find somebody (hopefully not anytime soon!), she will be lucky to have found either of my sons.

How can I serve as both the mother and the father figure?

I knew from day one that I had to act as a very strong, independent, tough, and capable person. Or at least I had to present that image to my boys. No matter how much I was struggling with my personal issues, I wanted them to see me as a calm and in-control person. I have always been conscious of the example I am setting. I could not have my boys shrieking like I used to when I saw a lizard, or jumping at the slightest bump in the night. Admittedly, I was not hesitant to jump and shriek when I was married, but now that they no longer have their father in their daily life, I cut it out. Just as I knew it was up to me to show them how to be gentlemanly, I also knew it was up to me to show them how to be tough. I have to say, I love being a mom to two boys. It fills me with this powerful coolness. I have never in my life known more about sports! A few techniques I have outlined for parenting the boys by myself, include:

1. I take them to the batting cage every week, and I get in the batting cage too. I bought myself two pairs of batting gloves (they are baby pink!), and I proudly give myself blisters alongside Cristian and Ryan.
2. I made sure I did not let myself show fear or sadness when they had to be hospitalized. No matter how fearful I was inside, I stayed by their bedsides, and I stayed strong.
3. I act as calm as possible when they are throwing up. Maybe too calm! My oldest son throws up when he gets excited, so

one time when he was opening his Christmas presents, he vomited on the floor and he acted as if he had just sneezed. He moved to the other side of the floor while I cleaned up, and he continued opening presents.

4. Baseball! I have them enrolled in baseball, and we watch the Yankees on TV. I am not sure this has anything to do with my trying to be a father figure, though. I think it comes from my blood. When I was growing up in Puerto Rico, baseball was always very important!

5. I will never say no if they ask me to build spaceships with LEGOS, play with action heroes, or have mini-car races.

6. I got them guitar lessons and drum lessons. Maybe the drums in the house were not the greatest idea, especially since they are right in front of my bedroom—it is definitely not the most soothing alarm clock.

7. I watch all the classic "boy movies" with them: E.T., Ninja Turtles, the whole StarWars collection, Indiana Jones. Then we dressed up as Darth Vader, Anakin, and Princess Leia for Halloween.

8. I let them be while they play on the backyard playground. It is tough on me. They run around with that wonderful carelessness that boys have. They jump from one side to the other like monkeys, they power down the slide headfirst, and they leap off the swings. And I keep my mouth shut . . . though I think it has taken years off of my life watching them on that playground!

What is the hardest part of parenting alone?

The hardest part is definitely disciplining the boys on my own. I am such a kid myself, and I am a playful mom. I cannot wait for the weekend so that we can go out and have fun! I love nothing more than taking the kids to the park, the movies, or baseball games where I scream like a lunatic. Or on rainy days, we will sit on the floor and do arts and crafts, make highways with all of our empty toilet-paper rolls, or have marathon Uno sessions. I have to say, I am great at being fun. I am not so great at being firm. When it comes time for discipline, it is hard for me, especially because there is no "wait until your father gets home"! It is all on me!

I had to read so many parenting books to help me be stronger and react the right way. I realize that discipline is just as important as fun. That's life, and I am not going to let my children lack discipline just because it does not come naturally to me. So I am still reading those books, and I still have many flaws that I have to work on, but I am getting better!

From Jinny

How do I know when I am ready to move into Rediscovery?

Getting back into life after divorce can seem like an overwhelming task. After all, it's a lot easier to stay inside and not have to worry about making any changes in your life. But by making an effort and moving forward, you get the chance to experience so much more in your life.

You can never find the perfect moment to make a change. However once you have worked on fortifying your foundation as a person, you will be eager to start rediscovering your life. Although taking control sometimes can make you feel scared, the excitement and expectation of all the wonderful things that will come to your life will help you overcome that feeling.

Use the tools that you learned in the Rebuilding phase, getting in touch with yourself and reading your own cues, to help you identify when you are ready to move on. You will know when you are ready!

Since the Acceptance phase is about accepting the situation, and the Rebuilding phase is about you, is the Rediscovery phase a combination of these two?

Absolutely. The Acceptance phase is about getting in touch with the situation. The Rebuilding phase is about getting in touch with you. The Rediscovery phase is about getting in touch with the world.

In this phase, you are bringing a new YOU into life so that you can rediscover your roles, hobbies, and dreams. In the Rebuilding phase, you were basically working on rebuilding the base of your building (your foundation), to make it strong, solid, and healthy. Now, in the Rediscovery phase, you are ready to build a tower on top of that strong foundation. This is the phase that gives you the opportunity to design your life in new and different ways.

How do I keep myself from getting stuck in any one step of the Rediscovery process?

When in the Rediscovery phase, you need to understand that the four steps are crucial to making a change. However, you may find that the steps to change will not always follow in a perfect sequence. You may find that you have to go back and revisit your preparation step in order to adjust your action stages or even your initial. It is okay. This is not a failure. This represents the nature and bravery of making changes. It is not an easy task, but when you reach each goal, you will have the most powerful feeling that will help you continue on the road to a beautiful life and take on your next goal.

Is it okay and healthy to feel that I do not ever want to get married again?

It is perfectly okay. It is just a result of having a hurtful experience. Again, when we get married we are definitely not thinking about getting divorced. On the contrary, we dream about getting old to-gether, supporting each other, maybe traveling around the world, or maybe having children. When these dreams do not come true, you become apprehensive about everything related to "marriage," because you have been so disillusioned.

This is completely normal because you are reacting after a not-so-pleasant experience. It is a cause-and-effect relationship. For instance, if you go to a restaurant and the food was not good, and maybe the service was not good either, would you go to that restaurant again? Probably not (unless you are a glutton for punishment). Does that mean that you would never try to go out to eat?

Something to remember is that "marriage" is not the issue; the issue is that the relationship with a partner, in the end, did not work. In fact, maybe you will change your opinion regarding getting married again or not when the "right" person comes along. . . . (Nunca digas nunca. . . .)

And how do I deal with people who ask when I am going to get married again?

As mentioned throughout the phases, the way you handle questions and situations with those around you will set the stage for how everyone else will continue to act. You do not have to give explanations to justify what you think. You can say yes, no, or I am not thinking about that right now. Regardless of the answer, you just need to say it and move on; this will let everybody know that your life is not based around "marriage." They could be thinking only about marriage when they see you or talk about you because you were once so content with the institution of marriage and you wanted nothing more than to settle down with a partner. They may feel that if you just married again, you will be happy. What these friends and family may not realize is that the amazing transformation you are going through after divorce is making you happy in ways nobody else can fully understand.

How do I avoid being too fearful in my new relationships? (For example: If I was too passive in my marriage, perhaps I will try to go too far the other way and be controlling and demanding.)

The capacity to learn from experiences is one of the beauties of being a human being. Yes, you may want to try new things and behave in different ways; however, learning from an experience does not mean that you will do the exact opposite of what you did before. You need to know who you are when entering a new relationship, but you also need to know the areas that you would like to improve that are healthy and meaningful for you and your new relationship.

You do not need to change your persona in order to have a successful relationship. You need to be true to yourself and, yes, adjust some areas that you want to improve. If you were the woman who always gave up the remote, always let her partner choose what she ate for dinner, and never voiced her frustrations, take note of this and try to remind yourself to adjust these behaviors. Learn to communicate your wants, needs, and frustrations in a healthy way. But you do not need to go to the extreme and turn yourself into someone else. Just because you were too passive in your past relationship does not mean you should monopolize your new relationship. Life and relationships should be about balance. Share the remote. Share the dinner decisions.

How do I deal with people who are always shaking my foundations and trying to halt my Rediscovery, especially when I love them (for example, my mother, sister, or best friend)?

You need to understand that you do not instantly live inside a "crystal ball" where your life and foundation are protected and where nobody or nothing can disturb you. However, you can build elements of that "crystal ball" around you. It is okay, and healthy, to listen to other points of view, but DO NOT let that shake your foundation. In those cases where they give you advice without you asking for it, you just need to listen to what they are saying (even though you may not agree), do not argue, and move on. Try to avoid discussing areas of your life with those who have strong and contrary opinions as to how you should live your life. The only person who understands exactly what is happening in your life is you!

You are the director of a movie (your life), and you should picture every day as you would direct a scene that is going to make that movie. You have a crew of people who will guide you in specific areas, and they will all give you advice, telling you how they think each scene would work best. These people are crucial components of the project, but they should not change the vision of your movie. Ultimately, because you are the director, it is your call on how to proceed.

Is it okay to do nothing some days?

It is perfectly fine to have some "down days," when you just want to recharge, especially after surviving such an intense roller coaster of emotions. However, what matters is when and how.

WHEN: You definitely do not want to have these days when you are not emotionally ready. For instance, if you feel a little sad, you need to get active and engage in activities that will help you feel happy and energetic.

HOW: How you have "down days" is crucial. Make sure you do something you like when you are having one of those "do-nothing days." You don't want to just stare at the ceiling. Watch your favorite movies, read a good book, or take a long bubble bath. Identify things that you enjoy doing so that even when you are "doing nothing," you are doing something that makes you feel good.

These days are effective when you just want to relax, take a break, and recharge your batteries, but they are not effective when you are not emotionally ready. You can hurt yourself if you are feeling depressed and doing things that promote the sadness and depression.

How do you deal with the fact that sometimes you feel like you have "lost?" (You feel your ex has fully healed, moved on, etc., and you are still getting STUCK every once in a while.)

Before dealing with those feelings, you need to understand them. Understand that you might have lost your partner, but you have NOT lost your life. Regardless of the intensity of the experience, you have learned a lot, and you are a better person for it. Understand that you are human and have feelings. Getting stuck every once in a while is not the issue, but having the necessary tools to effectively deal with that is. Know that it is not time alone or new love alone that is going to help you get over these sad feelings. You have to investigate yourself and what is at the root of your feelings in order to address them!

Understand that you have not lost, but you have won a lot. You have won because you were able to end a relationship that was not working, you have learned from that experience, and you have rediscovered yourself. You have won because you are able to look for your happiness.

What are the key elements to remember about each of the three phases?

Phases	What is it about?	Most important part	Key element
Acceptance (I)	Getting in touch with reality	FORGIVENESS	Accept and allow yourself to grieve
Rebuilding (II)	Getting in touch with yourself	YOU	Integration of yourself; getting to know yourself
Rediscovery (III)	Getting in touch with the world	Your LIFE	Life is FAIR!!!

Part Five

Letters from Friends

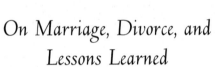

On Marriage, Divorce, and
Lessons Learned

"Turn your wounds into wisdom."
—Oprah Winfrey

When I started to write this book, I asked a few of my friends if they would want to write a few sentences regarding their divorces and what they have learned from them. I thought that they could touch on issues that I may not have experienced. Each of these friends had a different divorce experience and wanted to make sure that we covered as many "divorce issues" as possible. I asked these friends to write a just few sentences, but most of them wrote pages. I have pulled out the most touching, important, and useful pieces of their letters for you so that you can learn from their experiences and also realize that *you are not alone.*

KIM

Married for 7 years, divorced four years ago, no children

Well, I was married for seven years and luckily never had children. My ex asked for a divorce after he had long decided that our marriage was over. Apparently my job had been a large factor in making that decision for him. I traveled often, and he didn't say anything until it was much too late. He had already mentally and emotionally removed himself from the marriage and decided for the both of us that it was over. By that time, I honestly did not have a choice in the matter.

I have now been divorced for four years. I have had a real hard time in dealing with it. I am a private and discreet person as it is, and with the humiliation and embarrassment, I just shut down. I was paralyzed for a quite a while. I sometimes think I still am. I became angry and depressed. The thoughts of not wanting to be here came often. (They don't any longer.) But I was either angry or depressed—one or the other—every day for over two years. I still fall into that trap occasionally. My divorce ignited this fire in my gut. I have a lot of anger and really don't know how to deal with it. I have little patience and my temper is out of control. I become enraged by the smallest, most insignificant things. The rudeness of a bank teller or someone cutting me off in traffic just sets me off to no end. I also didn't tell my family members or friends about the divorce until I came home for Christmas dinner and well . . . he didn't.

What started out as an uncontested divorce quickly changed when I came across some items that did not belong to me. I do believe that things happen for a reason. Since the divorce, I have been able to do the job I love and travel to many different destinations, another love of mine. However, I lost something in the divorce too. I think I lost my trust in men or people in general. I still find it very hard to let anyone in. Or at least anyone new.

I have been going to a therapist for over a year now. I am taking baby steps in dealing with the divorce, among other things. I know he has moved on. I often say that I am ready, but anytime an opportunity arises, I make excuses. The thing is, he did just as he promised he wouldn't. His father cheated on his mother when he was a young teen. Having experienced and survived the hurt, he swore he wouldn't or couldn't do that to anyone. Well, my friends, the apple doesn't fall far from the tree.

As I said before, I believe that things happen for reasons to which we may never know the answers. So I am now comfortable with blanket statements in disclosing that I am divorced, but I don't express my deep thoughts or emotions concerning how I feel about it. Until now, that is. I have often pushed any serious thought off to the side, figuring it would somehow miraculously work itself out on its own if I just waited it out. It hasn't. I guess, in short, I am still hurt. I feel rejected and wonder if anyone will love me or if I will ever love anyone again. I lost my self-esteem. I lost my identity and I lost me. I don't know who I am and I don't know what makes me happy. I am just learning some of those things now. I do feel that I need to figure myself out before I let someone in, but I long to have someone special in my life. I know it will take a while to reach a place in which I am comfortable. There was a lot of damage done. I have not figured out, per se, what good came of this quite yet. I am still waiting for answers.

I do know that I don't miss him, but I do miss a person on the other end. I know in time it will change, but time can take forever. I just don't know if I can wait that long.

TRACEY
Married for 7½ years, divorced 1½ years ago, 2 children

Michael and I were married for just under 7½ years and dated for one year prior to that. He asked me to marry him, and bang, three months later we were married. We have two beautiful daughters, six and four. Because of them, I will NEVER regret our marriage!

We have been separated for a little over 1½ years and the divorce was final three months ago. I have to say it has been the hardest 1½ years of my life. It is as if someone put my life in a blender and it is on high all of the time. You have to love your friends that say to you, "My husband never helps. I am like a single mom." No, you really aren't. It is hard, and if you haven't been there, then you don't get it.

Our divorce was my decision. We had what I will call "an incident." Two days later, I was in the divorce attorney's office. I filed and never looked back. Though, honestly, I do mourn family, couples, family trips, family dinners, and so forth. All of this is the stuff you do not think about when you walk into your attorney's office. Fortunately for me, the divorce process was easy and we do get along now, which is so important for our daughters! So what have I learned? Definitely stay away from putting on twenty-five pounds. It's really hard to take off! Take care of yourself first and foremost; otherwise you cannot properly care for your children or anyone else.

EVELYN
Married for 10 years, 2 children

I was married for ten years and have two children from that marriage. The decision of getting divorced was a long and hard one because I was raised with traditional and conservative values. The prospect of being scrutinized by my own family was discouraging. Raising children on my own has been the toughest aspect of the divorce. Although I have been blessed with wonderful children, taking on the responsibilities of both parents has been challenging. Another difficult aspect of the divorce was on an emotional side. It hurt me to see my children sad. My children would question why this had happened to them. They were exposed to their friends' questions as to the absence of their dad.

What I have learned from this experience is that it has revealed to me an inner strength that I never knew I had before.

·MITCH

Married for 10 years, 2 kids

My story goes like this: When I met my wife in college, she claimed we were soul mates. After ten years, we split—no court, no lawyers, simple mutual respect, and a shared goal of moving on as peacefully as possible. For years after the end of the relationship, our two kids went back and forth between our homes every night. Sounds crazy, but it kinda worked. We lived around the block from each other and remained good friends. We're still good friends, but we've moved further apart—she's gotten remarried—I have a third child and a new relationship. We still share custody, but the schedule has become less back and forth. I do not consider myself a poster child for an ordered life, if such a thing even exists, but I can say that my kids, our crazy extended family, and I have large amounts of happiness and love. So what have I learned? If you can let go of "what could have been" and focus on "what is," you tend to be much better off.

OMAR

Married for 2 years, recently filed for divorced, 1 child

I met my ex-wife in 2003 and we dated for seven months. I knew right away that she was not the one for me. After seven months, we broke up and decided to remain friends. I went on location to shoot a film, and two weeks later she called me to say that she was pregnant. When the filming wrapped, I went back to Miami to speak with her father. I told him that I wasn't ready to get married. We were still very young and needed to get to know each other more. I told him that I wanted to live together to see how it worked out. He told me that was out of the question and that if I did not marry his daughter, she could not live with me. I did what I thought was the right thing and I asked her to marry me. During this time I discovered that she had had a very tumultuous childhood and suffered severe panic attacks as a result. We grew very close as we tried to work through all of her fears and troubles.

When our little girl was born, it was the best thing that has ever happened to me. We decided that we should move to Los Angeles so that I could pursue my acting career. I flew out to look for a place for us to live, and I planned to return to Miami to pick them up and take them back to California. When I got back to Miami, I discovered that she had been unfaithful. We separated for some time, but I eventually decided that we should try again for the sake our daughter. We got back together and moved to LA and lived there for three or four months. It was only a matter of time before she lied again, and that is when I decided to file for divorce in the Los Angeles courts. I could not take the deceptions anymore. She moved to Miami and filed for divorce there under her mother's address and stating that Florida was our daughter's state of residence.

Things have gotten uglier and uglier. I will not go into all of the details, but the short story is that I am in a horrible custody battle. The part that bothers me most is that I know that my daughter is not in a stable environment and there is nothing I can do about it. I feel like I am the only one who is thinking of my daughter's feelings and how all of this will affect her. I am still at the center of the storm, so I am not sure that I have learned much from my divorce at this point. I do know that adults should not hurt each other through their own children as revenge, and I hope and pray that my ex-wife realizes that before it is too late.

ELSA
Married 21 months, 1 child

I was married for a year and nine months to a man who initially seemed tender and loving, but who later changed into a dominant, aggressive, and abusive person.

When we were dating, I saw signs of aggressiveness in him, but since he never hit me, I attributed them to work-related stress and the challenge of adapting to our new life together. But little by little, he began to show who he really was: a cold, calculating, abusive, and imposing human being.

After a year and six months of marriage and two attempted separations, I got pregnant with my "salvation," Fabian. I was flooded with conflicting emotions . . . happiness, confusion, and worry. Who would have thought that after wishing so much for a child, I would feel such worry and guilt for bringing a child into a home where physical, verbal and emotional abuse was a daily occurrence? It made me feel like the worst mother.

But it was precisely Fabian who gave me the strength to leave that sickening relationship, where "Sorry," "I will never do it again," "I love you," "You are my everything," and "You provoked it because you didn't do as I told you" were daily proclamations that did not allow me to see the reality of my situation. It was for Fabian's sake, as well as my own, that I decided to exit that relationship that had harmed me so much, and would also harm my baby if I did not make my decision quickly enough.

It was not easy for me to leave. I had to call an 800 help line for victims of domestic violence and call the police in order to get him out of the house, since I made the decision in the middle of an incident that put the life of my baby at risk (and maybe mine, as well).

There were many times when depression, confusion, and tears overwhelmed me. I suffered, yes, a lot. When I got married I believed it would be for the rest of my life. I dreamed of having a loving home and one or two kids filling it with happiness.

But the reality was entirely different. I was alone (in a city far from my country), pregnant (for the first time), unemployed (because I worked for him), and with more worry and uncertainty than I had ever had in my life. Will I be able to raise my child on my own? Yes, I can! God has been with me at all times, and I know it because He has given me an amazing son who each day gives me the strength to stand up and strive for a better future for both of us.

I really never let myself fall down. Life's blows and all the suffering have made me a mature woman, intelligent and sure of herself, who proudly walks with her head held high because even though I put up with and allowed many negative things in my relationship, it was exactly those things that made me react, acknowledge my reality, and make the right decision.

Eight years have passed, and I have to admit that when I remember all of the suffering and pain I went through, I can't help but cry. I don't know why, but I cry. It still hurts me. Maybe I have not gotten over it yet. . . . I don't know. But the one thing I am absolutely certain about is that today I am the happy mother of a beautiful and loving boy who adores me and lets me know it all the time; who makes me the most beautiful drawings and love letters; who I am crazy in love with; and who I call my "my little love."

Fabian and I have a peaceful, beautiful, and safe life and excellent communication. It is not easy raising a child by oneself. As a single mom who works outside the home, I alone am responsible for everything having to do with homework, grades, situations that arise with classmates (my son is being evaluated for attention deficit disorder), in addition to dealing with all the home-maintenance issues, the bills, and financial responsibilities (we don't receive child support).

As a mom, I always try to give my son the very best of me, and though at times I may get frustrated by situations that arise, I know I am doing a good job. I know that I will one day see my son go very far. He will be a professional and a man of integrity. I believe in him—and in myself too!

I learned not to be afraid of expressing my true feelings, to make my own decisions, and not to allow into my life anything that I do not desire. I have realized that I am stronger than I ever thought I could be.

SARAH

Married for 5 years, considering divorce, 1 child

I have been married for five years and have been blessed with the daughter of our dreams. We are currently attending weekly therapy sessions that were originally meant to help repair our marriage. Instead they have served to convince me that what I want most is to live on my own with my daughter; that though I love my husband dearly, I am not in love with him; and further, that try as he might, he simply does not have the capacity to be the life partner I need to be happy now and in the future.

All my life, I have wanted to be a mom. Though I am a successful career woman, it is not exactly what I aspired to be. I simply wanted to be a mom to two children who would have the wonderful father I never had. I became driven to graduate from college and excel at work because of what I had experienced in my home. My mom lived in a nightmare of a marriage mostly because she depended on my father financially, and I vowed never to be in that situation. I grew up protecting my mom from my physically and emotionally abusive father (who was also a womanizer) and begging her every single day to leave him (and call the police!!). It was painful to see my mother so unhappy, but she felt she had to stay with my dad because of her children and because of financial stability. So growing up, I was the adult and the nurturer at home, and my mom was always a nervous wreck. Though I spent wonderful summers away at camp, I don't remember having much of a childhood. When my parents finally divorced after twenty-five years of marriage, I could not have been more relieved.

When it came time for me to choose a life partner, all I wanted was the opposite of my dad. "A good guy," with a kind heart, who was faithful, respectful, low-key, and who would never resort to violence (verbally or physically). My mom would always say, "You need to marry someone wealthy so he can take care of you," and "It is just as easy to fall in love with a rich man as with a poor man," which at the time, I thought were shallow and disgusting statements. Besides, I thought, I can make my own living, so I can marry anyone I fall in love with, regardless of his income.

When I finally met, dated, and married my very nice husband, I thought it was the beginning of a wonderful life together. How could we go wrong? He was a good guy!! I was so in love that I was happy just being in the same room with him. I thrived on taking care of everything, and loving and nurturing him. It never occurred to me that I also needed to be taken care of. He is successful in an artistic career that requires a lot of travel and is extremely unstable; even the best artists can struggle financially. His art is not just his career; it is his greatest passion, his LIFE—something I initially thought was beautiful and admirable.

We bought a house together with a down payment I put down. I bought our car because his was a used one from the eighties. And we started our life as husband and wife. I handled everything while he was on the road working. The first year was fine, because I am very independent and I welcomed the time to myself, but by year two I could tell we were becoming disconnected. When I got pregnant for the first time, his reaction was to complain about the things we didn't get to do together before the pregnancy. It was a tough and depressing pregnancy that I spent mainly alone (because he was on the road), and I lost the baby at nineteen weeks. Of course, I was alone when I lost her as well.

I now believe that at that point, deep down, I already knew we were in trouble, but I was so obsessed with having a child that I did not dare acknowledge it. Plus, he was a good guy who loved me and was faithful, and everyone raved about how devoted he was and how lucky we were to have such a great relationship.

A few months later I got pregnant again. Once again, during the pregnancy, I was fraught with worry and depression, and again, I spent it mostly alone, working nonstop and taking care of everything at home. My husband was there for the birth, but even though I begged him not to, when my daughter was only ten days old, he left town on business for two months. So I was left alone with a newborn, in a city with no family and no nanny to help me . . . and I was still working full-time. I never took a single week of maternity leave.

By the time my daughter turned one, I came to the realization that I was not happy, and that for the last three years, I had actually been a very depressed woman. I also started to realize that with all of the responsibilities of being the primary bread winner and the primary caregiver to my child, I was a nervous wreck, always stressed-out and anxiety-ridden, not myself, not LIVING, just existing. If I didn't do something about it soon, I was not going to be able to be the best mom I could be for my precious child.

As I opened my eyes to the reality of my situation, I became increasingly angry and resentful. Why did this great man I married, who loved me so much, also neglect me so much? Why didn't he understand that he needed to at least try to become the main provider for our family, especially when I always said my dream was to be a mom, first and foremost? Why didn't he feel a need to be there for us or even be present when he did happen to be around. Why were we not a priority? How could I have spent the last three years of my life depressed (and believe me, it was *obvious*), and he didn't even address it, try to make me feel better, or be there for me?

I suddenly saw things exactly as they were. Though he is a nice man who is faithful and means well, he also lacks the capacity to be someone who is an equal partner with me, someone who can make our family a priority. His actions demonstrated that he was happy to have me sacrifice my dreams (of being a full-time mom and having another child) so that I could continue to work hard to ensure he could live out his dream life, year after year. He could continue to work on his craft, traveling around the world, while he had the perfect wife and child waiting for him in his perfect little home.

I have even come to believe that my husband was in love with the idea of the marriage, of what it was perceived to be, and how it made him feel. I am not so sure he was in love with me, simply because he never devoted the love and attention necessary to make things work. He seemed content to have our family on automatic pilot, and that became unacceptable to me.

I have decided we need to separate, but my husband still hopes the marriage can be saved. He is now willing to do "whatever it takes" to make things work, but I feel it is way too late. The positive side is that the situation has made him a more hands-on dad, and he has finally bonded with our daughter. They adore each other, and it is beautiful to see.

I feel terrible about what I am doing to him, especially because he will have to live away from our baby girl, but I have promised myself to be fair and allow him as much time as necessary with her, even if it hurts me to be away from her on the days that she will be with him. I still feel she can have the wonderful father I never had, even if we are not married. I also know that it would be unhealthy for our daughter to see her mother living an unhappy existence (as I saw with my mother).

I want her to know the ME I used to be. The happy, energetic, full-of-life, adventurous ME. I also want her to get to know the ME I have become—a woman who is nurturing to others, but also takes care of herself; a woman who finally knows what she is worth and will not settle for less than what she deserves; a woman who has realized that only by being emotionally healthy and happy can she be the very best mother for her daughter.

I know it will not be easy, and I will go through many struggles and feel guilty, but I know it is the best decision for my daughter and myself.

What I have learned so far:

I have learned that you need a partner who is willing and able to grow and face life's challenges together, and who believes in values and supports your dreams as much as you support his.

I have learned that you need to be the very best YOU and be emotionally healthy and happy to be the very best mom and role model, even if achieving this requires getting a divorce.

I have learned that it is absolutely okay to think about yourself and do what you need to do to be happy.

I have learned that though divorce is incredibly hard, especially when you have children, it also creates an opportunity to start fresh and to create a new and more happy and fulfilling life for you and your child.

JAVIER
Married for 5 years, 2 children

We were together for more than sixteen years. We always felt that marriage was not an essential institution, and we formed our family out of wedlock. Then one day our youngest son bombarded us with questions about why we were not married; and without thinking about it much, we decided to take that step to legitimize our union after eleven years of living together.

There were many extremely happy occasions that made us momentarily forget that we already had many dysfunctions in our relationship. It had been a long time since we had been intimate, and perhaps the worst error on my part was not ever bringing up the subject and dealing with it with a specialist who would have helped us better understand the different stages couples go through when they swear to be together "until death do us part."

On one side I would fill the lack of sex, cheating on my wife on my frequent business trips. On the other side my wife would treat me rudely and even with a lack of respect when we were at gatherings with friends, in order to unleash her frustrations. Instead of placing limits on her attitude toward me, I would choose to say nothing because of the deep sense of guilt I had felt ever since the first time I was unfaithful.

As you can imagine, this went from bad to worse, until one day my wife asked me if I had ever been unfaithful. I clumsily tried to avoid the subject, but in the midst of the argument, I decided to liberate myself, and I confessed that I had been unfaithful several times.

That was the end of our relationship as a couple. After we simmered down from all that was said and done, I was able to communicate with her once again, but we were never able to reconcile because the trust was gone.

The positive that came out of this bad story is that we learned to respect each other and to take care of our family as our main priority. Today, we have been able to reach a level of friendship that has allowed us to enjoy each other's company as friends. We still have to see what will happen when she or I appear with a significant other by our side. This story will continue.

My Final Words

"Every ending is a new beginning."
—*Proverb*

I made the decision that I was going to move to LA in spring 2004. Miami had been my safe haven for two years; it was the place where I had become solid and stable and strong. I had a tremendous support system there, but in ways that only I can understand, I also knew that I had to leave this support system behind. I had to be my own support system for a little while. I told Jennifer to start looking for an apartment since she was already living in LA. She kept saying, "Are you sure?" And I was. I have never been so sure of anything in my life. Jinny was pregnant with Andrea at the time, and I decided that after Andrea was born, I would spend a month with Jinny, and then I was going to go.

In September 2005, I arrived in LA, and it just felt right. For the first few months, we lived in a tiny, cramped apartment. Well, everyone tells me it was tiny and cramped, but I don't remember it like that. I remember it being wonderful. The living room, dining room, and kitchen were the size of my former bedroom, but I loved it so much more. It was mine, all mine. I remember the boys constantly being on top of me, and I was responsible for every minute of every day. It felt amazing. We would go out and explore the city for hours; we were a merry band of three children delighting in the fact that everything was exciting and new. We all fell in love with the city right away. I didn't call back to Miami as much as I thought I would or maybe even should have. It was as though Jinny had been my college course, and then she let me fly. She knew me well enough and loved me deep enough to let me go. I had her unrelenting support and then her unrelenting release, which are the best gifts a friend, a sister, or a therapist can give.

Two years after I made my move, I got a call from Jinny telling me that she and Jose were thinking about moving out to LA. I did not let myself get excited. I did not let myself think that it was really going to happen. It was too good to be true. Yet, a few weeks ago, in the middle of our writing this book, Jinny, Jose, and Andrea really did move out here. I feel as though my life has come full circle. Just days ago, as we were going over our edits for the book, Jinny and I sat hip to hip as we did so many years ago on our bed in Puerto Rico as young girls. We giggled. We reminisced. We discussed life and love. We talked not about wedding dresses, but about divorces, new relationships, and old loves. We also talked about where we were when we had gotten engaged. I was in a walk-in closet. Jinny was backstage at a concert. I'm pretty sure that wasn't how we foresaw our proposals all those years ago as teenage girls planning out our futures.

But really, nothing that we predicted or had planned came true. I never dreamed I'd be Miss Universe. I never thought I would end up divorced. Neither of us ever thought we'd live in LA. Neither of us ever thought we'd write a book. And yet here we are. Life took us by the hand and led us to this amazing place. If I had to do it all over again to get to this place, sitting hip to hip with my best friend, giggling, reminiscing, talking about life and love, I can say with absolute certainty I'd do it all exactly the same.

It has been eight years since I said, "I do," and four years since I said, "Goodbye." It has taken me four full years to move through Acceptance and Rebuilding, and finally to get to the Rediscovery. I am fully committed to the Rediscovery phase, and I don't want to ever move out of it. This was the biggest mistake I made in my marriage. I stopped searching myself; I stopped letting myself grow. I believe that we are put on earth to find our own happiness and to continually rediscover ourselves. If we are lucky enough to find partners to help us in our quests, we should hold on to them tight, and in turn we should help them in their quests. But as soon as we start holding one another down, as soon as we start spending our days trying to survive bad days, instead of thriving and creating happiness, we should let one another go.

Getting a divorce was the most difficult decision I have ever made, but I have come to realize that it was also the most mature decision I have ever made. Out of respect for myself, my children, and my ex-husband, I could no longer keep us all in that marriage.

Today, I am proud to say that I am married to a great woman. Her name is Dayanara. Yari, for short. She is beautiful and fun and intelligent. She is a great mother, a great friend, a great sister and daughter. She has goals and aspirations, and she is not about to let anyone take them away from her. She doesn't look back on the past with regret; she looks to the future with hope and excitement.

I know that you and I have not had the same divorce experiences, nor have we had the same marriage experiences. Our goals, wishes, and desires may be completely different, but I hope that you can use my story as an inspiration. I hope that you will be able to discover the person you always wanted to be and that you can stand with me, on stable ground, gazing out to the horizon, ready to walk toward the future in a solid, stable relationship . . . with yourself.

A Few of My Favorite Things

M y goal was to drop all of the baggage from my divorce and carry around one very chic, very useful
bag of items. In this bag, I stowed some of the
books that I loved, the movies that inspired me, and the music
that inspired me to scream at the top of my lungs in the car. Here
are my lists, which I am constantly adding to. . . .

THE BOOKS

I could not find a divorce handbook I liked, but I did find things to
read. I read books for strength, for escape, and for parenting advice.

> **A Reading List for Strength**
> 1. *The Secret* by Rhonda Byrne
> 2. *Chocolate for a Mother's Heart* by Kay Allenbaugh
> 3. *A Woman's Worth* by Marianne Williamson

4. *After the Breakup* by Angela Watrous and Carole Honeychurch
5. *A Woman's Guide to Getting Through Tough Times* by Quin Sherrer and Ruthanne Garlock
6. *Why Men Love Bitches* by Sherry Argov
7. *When I Loved Myself Enough* by Kim McMillen
8. *God Is in the Small Stuff* by Bruce Bickel and Stan Jantz
9. *The Game of Life and How to Play It* by Florence Scovel-Shinn
10. *The Book of Secrets* by Deepak Chopra
11. *In the Meantime* by Iyanla Vanzant

A Reading List for Escape

1. *The Princess Who Believed in Fairy Tales* by Marcia Grad
2. *Heartburn* by Nora Ephron
3. *Tart* by Jody Gehrman
4. *A Hundred Years of Solitude* by Gabriel García Márquez
5. *Pride and Prejudice* by Jane Austen
6. *Persuasion* by Jane Austen
7. *The Cocktail Party* by T. S. Eliot
8. *The Alchemist* by Paulo Coelho
9. *Like Water for Chocolate* Laura Esquivel
10. *Chocolat* by Joanne Harris
11. *Eat, Pray, Love* by Elizabeth Gilbert

A Reading List for Mothers

1. *The Hot Mom's Handbook* by Jessica Denay
2. *Why a Son Needs a Mom* by Gregory E. Lang
3. *First-Time Mom* by Dr. Kevin Leman
4. *Raising Boys* by Steve Biddulph
5. *Perfect Parenting* by Elizabeth Pantley
6. *Supernanny* by Jo Frost

7. Bringing Up Boys by Dr. James Dobson
8. The Busy Mom's Book of Preschool Activities by Jamie Kyle McGillian and with illustrations by Tracey Wood
9. The Everything Parent's Guide to the Strong-Willed Child by Carl E. Pickhardt, PhD
10. The Power of Positive Talk by Jon Merritt and Douglas Bloch
11. 100 Promises to My Baby by Mallika Chopra
12. Chicken Soup for the Working Mom's Soul by Jack Canfield, Mark Hansen, and Patty Aubery
13. I Was a Really Good Mom Before I Had Kids by Trisha Ashworth and Amy Nobile

$\mathscr{T}$HE MOVIES

No matter the story line, these are movies that I think lift your spirit, transport you, and for a time make you forget what you are going through. They will leave you with a sense of happiness, independence, and power!

1. Amélie
2. Love Story
3. Cinderella Man
4. Mary Poppins
5. Funny Face
6. The Way We Were
7. Breakfast at Tiffany's
8. Not Without My Daughter
9. Love Actually
10. The Secret

11. The Devil Wears Prada
12. Charade
13. Roman Holiday
14. My Fair Lady
15. Waitress
16. The Joy Luck Club
17. Where the Heart Is
18. The Little Princess
19. Women on the Verge of a Nervous Breakdown

The Music

Thank God for tinted windows and patient friends, because I drove around belting these songs out as if I was Céline Dion.

Sound Track One: A New Day
1. "Bring on the Rain," Jo Dee Messina
2. "A New Day," Céline Dion
3. "I Will Love Again," Lara Fabian
4. "Lessons Learned," Carrie Underwood
5. "All by Myself," Céline Dion
6. "Wasted," Carrie Underwood
7. "Was That My Life?" Jo Dee Messina
8. "I Will Survive," Gloria Gaynor
9. "I Get Wings to Fly, I'm Alive," Céline Dion
10. "I Drove All Night," Céline Dion
11. "Stand Beside Me," Jo Dee Messina
12. "You Found Me," Kelly Clarkson
13. "Survivor," Destiny's Child

14. "Since You've Been Gone," Kelly Clarkson
15. "Breakaway," Kelly Clarkson
16. "Mr. Brightside," The Killers
17. "I'm Still Standing," Elton John
18. "Three Little Birds," Bob Marley
19. "Get Up, Stand Up," Bob Marley
20. "You're Beautiful," James Blunt
21. "Superwoman," Alicia Keys
22. "Taking Chances," Céline Dion
23. "I Am Who I Am," Lara Fabian
24. "Beautiful Now," Alex Woodard
25. "Unwritten," Natasha Bedingfield

Sound Track Two: For My Boys
1. "A New Day," Céline Dion
2. "The Greatest Reward," Céline Dion
3. "Have You Ever Been in Love?" Céline Dion
4. "I Hope You Dance," Lee Ann Womack
5. "If I Could," Céline Dion
6. "No One (I Just Want You Close)," Alicia Keys
7. "You and I," Céline Dion
8. "Breathe," Faith Hill
9. "Endless Love," Luther Vandross
10. "Imagine," John Lennon
11. "One Love," Bob Marley
12. "Is This Love," Bob Marley
13. "I Believe I Can Fly," R. Kelly
14. "Angel," Sarah McLachlan
15. "I'm Your Angel," Céline Dion

16. "A World to Believe In," Céline Dion
17. "Everything You Do," Marc Anthony

Sound Track Three: Karma
 1. "Irreplaceable," Beyoncé
 2. "Before He Cheats," Carrie Underwood
 3. "Wise Men," James Blunt
 4. "Lesson in Leaving," Jo Dee Messina
 5. "Too Little, Too Late," JoJo
 6. "What Goes Around," Justin Timberlake
 7. "Cry Me a River," Justin Timberlake
 8. "You'll Think of Me," Keith Urban
 9. "Because of You," Kelly Clarkson
10. "Gone," Kelly Clarkson
11. "There You Go," Pink
12. "Go Ahead," Alicia Keys
13. "Fade Away," Céline Dion
14. "Karma," Alicia Keys
15. "Apologize," One Republic

Sound Track Four: Magic Night, The Sad Soundtrack
 1. "Making Love out of Nothing at All," Air Supply
 2. "All out of Love," Air Supply
 3. "Do I Have to Say the Words?" Bryan Adams
 4. "I Do It For You," Bryan Adams
 5. "Hard to Say I'm Sorry," Chicago
 6. "If You Leave Me Now," Peter Cetera
 7. "Look Away," Chicago
 8. "Will You Still Love Me?" Chicago
 9. "You're the Inspiration," Chicago

10. "I Don't Wanna Live Without Your Love," Chicago
11. "If This Is the End," Faith Hill
12. "How to Save a Life," The Fray
13. "What About Love," Heart
14. "These Dreams," Heart
15. "Open Arms," Journey
16. "Here with Me," REO Speedwagon
17. "Keep on Loving You," REO Speedwagon
18. "Can't Fight This Feeling," REO Speedwagon
19. "Now and Forever," Richard Marx
20. "With or Without You," U2

Sound Track Five: Cry . . . and Let Go
1. "The Winner Takes It All," ABBA
2. "This Ain't a Love Song," Bon Jovi
3. "Jesus, Take the Wheel," Carrie Underwood
4. "Goodbye's (the Saddest Word)," Céline Dion
5. "Broken Vow," Lara Fabian
6. "You're Not from Here," Lara Fabian
7. "To Love Again," Lara Fabian
8. "Adagio," Lara Fabian
9. "My Heart Will Go On," Céline Dion
10. "Stronger," Faith Hill
11. "Alone," Heart
12. "Goodbye My Lover," James Blunt
13. "Faithfully," Journey
14. "Endless Summer Nights," Richard Marx
15. "Hold on to the Night," Richard Marx
16. "Right Here Waiting," Richard Marx

17. "Honestly," Stryper
18. "Alone," Céline Dion
19. "I Wish," Jo Dee Messina
20. "Starts with Goodbye," Carrie Underwood

THE FOOD

In Puerto Rico, there is no problem that we do not throw a plate of food at. When in doubt, we cook or we eat. I swear, it helps. After my divorce, Mom was always in my kitchen, making me my favorite food. The smells and tastes would transport me to my childhood, and I would immediately feel comforted. I had Mom write down (by force) her guidelines for my favorite Puerto Rican foods.

Mom's Recipes

Alitas (Chicken Wings)

A barbecue staple!

1 dozen chicken wings
1 tablespoon apple cider vinegar
adobo, oregano, garlic powder, and pepper, to taste

- Marinate the chicken with adobo, pepper, garlic, oregano, and vinegar mixture.
- Let stand for 15 minutes.
- Barbecue the chicken, making sure to continually turn the pieces. (You can also panfry, if a barbecue is not available.)
- Done when all the wings are golden.

Mofongo (Mashed Plantains)

3 green plantains
3 garlic cloves
1 teaspoon salt
4 cups water
1 tablespoon olive oil
½ pound crisp fried pork cracklings
Optional: fried bacon, lard, or vegetable oil

- Peel the plantains and cut them into one-inch slices.
- Soak the plantains for 15 minutes in salt and water, then drain.

- Fry the plantain slices for 15 minutes in hot oil (350°F), and then drain on paper towels.
- Pound the garlic cloves in a mortar, and sprinkle with the salt and add olive oil.
- Keep pounding.
- Crush the fried plantain slices and the pork; then add the garlic mixture.
- Keep pounding.
- Use a spoon to shape the mixture into two-inch balls.
- Place in an oven pan and keep warm until you are ready to serve.

Antipasto

1 tablespoon olive oil
½ onion (diced)
½ green pepper (diced)
8 ounces tomato sauce
6 Spanish olives (diced)
8-ounce can of sliced carrots (diced)
2 cans tuna (in water)
2–3 tablespoons catsup

- In a large pan, add the oil, onion, and pepper. Cook on medium heat until soft, mixing thoroughly.
- Add the tomato sauce, olives, carrots, and tuna, mixing thoroughly.
- Add the catsup, and mix.
- Let simmer for 30 seconds before taking off the heat.
- Let cool and then serve with Ritz crackers.

Asopao

14 cups water

1 chicken, cut in pieces

1 envelope Sazón Goya (con culantro y achiote)

1 envelope Sazón Accent (original)

1 cube chicken bouillon

8 ounces tomato sauce

2 tablespoons Spanish olives

½ onion (diced)

½ green pepper (diced)

3 cilantro leaves

2 culantro leaves

1 cup rice

salt to taste

4 ounces sweet red pimentos

- In a big pot, add the water, then the chicken, then the remaining ingredients (except the rice, salt, and pimentos), and bring to a boil.
- Once the water is boiling, add the rice and salt. Boil until the rice is soft.
- Remove from the heat and add the sweet pimentos.

Bacalaitos (Cod Fritters)

These always remind me of Sundays after church, and when I leave my church in LA, I still expect to see the bacalaitos vendor.

1 cup all-purpose flour

1 cod fish with no bones, diced

1 tablespoon oregano
2 cloves garlic (smashed)
1½ cups pilsner
oil for frying

• In a large bowl, mix the flour with the cod fish.
• Add the oregano, garlic, and beer.
• Heat oil (on medium heat) in a deep pan.
• When the oil is hot, add the mix by spoonfuls and fry until crispy.

Buñuelos (Fritters)

FOR THE FRITTERS
1 cup water
1 stick butter
½ teaspoon salt
1 cup all-purpose flour
4 eggs
oil for frying

FOR THE SYRUP
1 cup sugar
½ cup water
1 teaspoon vanilla

• Boil the cup of water with the butter and the salt.
• In a large bowl, place the cup of flour and start adding the water-butter mixture little by little and mix (do not beat).
• Add the eggs one by one and mix.
• When everything is well blended, add small spoon-sized amounts of batter to the frying pot.
• Turn the buñuelos when brown on one side.

- Take them out and put them on a paper towel to drain.
- Make the syrup by boiling the sugar, water, and vanilla for about 15 minutes and then let cool.
- When cool, dip the buñuelos into the syrup.

Ensalada de Coditos (Pasta Salad)

1 pound macaroni elbows
pinch salt
½ pound cooked ham (diced)
3 hard-boiled egges (diced)
½ onion (diced)
3 celery sticks (diced)
4 ounces sweet red pimentos (diced)
8 ounces mayonnaise

- Boil the macaroni with salt and drain when soft.
- In a large bowl, mix the macaroni and all of the diced ingredients, and refrigerate.
- When ready to eat, add the mayonnaise and mix well.

Arroz con Gandules (Rice and Pigeon Peas)

½ cup corn oil
½ pound bacon (chopped)
1 large can of gandules (green pigeon peas)
½ onion (diced)
½ green pepper (diced)
2 cloves garlic (smashed)
2 cilantro leaves

2 cilantro leaves
1 cube chicken bouillon
½ teaspoon oregano
1 envelope Sazón Goya (con culantro y achiote)
1 envelope Sazón Accent (original)
1 small green plantain (shredded)
2 cups rice
3 cups water
salt to taste

- In a large pot, heat the oil and then add the bacon.
- When the bacon is cooked, but not crisp, add the onion, green pepper, garlic, culantro and cilantro leaves, chicken bouillon, oregano, and the Sazón envelopes. Sauté.
- Add the plantain and mix.
- Add the rice, water, and salt.
- Let the mixture boil until it is dry. Stir, cover, turn to low heat, and cook for 30 minutes.
- Stir again and then serve.

Habichuelas (Stewed Beans)

16 ounces red kidney beans
½ can tomato sauce
½ envelope Sazón Goya (con culantro y achiote)
½ envelope Sazón Accent (original)
½ cube chicken bouillon
1 pound squash (cubed)
1 pound cooked ham (cubed)
salt to taste
¼ cup onion (diced)
¼ cup green pepper (diced)

¼ teaspoon oregano
2 cilantro leaves
2 culantro leaves
1½ cups water

Bring all the ingredients to a boil and continue to boil until the squash is soft.

Sandwichitos de Mezcla

A platter of these is mandatory at every child's birthday party.

16 ounces Cheese Whiz
12 ounces jamonilla
6 stuffed olives
10-ounce tin red pimentos
1 loaf white bread (crusts cut off)

• Mix all the ingredients except the bread in a blender or food processor.
• Spread the mixture onto the bread, make sandwiches, and then cut into four triangular pieces.

Limber de Coco (Coconut Ice)

This is my favorite dessert, and I am always impatient while waiting for it to freeze!

2 coconuts
6 cups water
3 cups sugar

- Crack the coconuts, remove the inside, and chop it up into cubes.
- In a blender, mix a portion of the coconut and about a cup of water.
- Pour the mixture into a cheese cloth and squeeze out the liquid into a separate jug. Discard the remaining coconut (but reserve a few tablespoons for later).
- Repeat the previous two steps until there is no more coconut left.
- Pour the liquid into plastic glasses or ice trays.
- Chop up the reserved coconut and place on top of the liquid.
- Freeze until firm.

Flan de Queso (Cheese Flan)

FOR THE CARAMEL

1 cup sugar

1 cup water

FOR THE CUSTARD

8 ounces cream cheese

12-ounce can evaporated milk

12-ounce can condensed milk

6 eggs

1 teaspoon vanilla

To Make the Caramel

- Boil the sugar and water until light brown.
- Pour into the flan pan so that it covers the bottom.

To Make the Custard

- Put all ingredients in a blender and mix until smooth.
- Pour the mixture into a flan mold.
- Place the flan mold into the larger pan and add water to the outer pan until almost full.
- Bake at 350°F for 1 hour.

Polvorones (Almond Cookies)

1 egg yolk
½ cup sugar
1 stick butter
1 teaspoon almond extract
1½ cups flour

- Preheat the oven to 350°F.
- Beat the egg yolks, sugar, butter, and almond extract in a large bowl.
- Mix in the flour a little at a time.
- Shape the dough into a tablespoon-sized balls.
- Bake on an ungreased cookie sheet for 20 minutes, or until golden.

Coquito (Puerto Rican Eggnog)

My favorite drink!

12-ounce can evaporated milk
12-ounce can cream of coconut
2 cans condensed milk
8 eggs
cinnamon, to taste
1 bottle light rum

- Mix all the ingredients except the rum in a blender.
- Put the mixture into a big bowl and add the rum.
- Chill!

My Recipes

Fried Crackers

We used to make these when I was younger. Because we had no money, I guess we had to make things interesting. So disgusting and so yummy!

crackers
new frying oil (you can't use old frying oil for this recipe)

- Pop the crackers into the frying oil for one minute.
- Remove and let cool a bit before eating.

Pie de Yari

My specialty!

24 ounces cream cheese
1 bag of mini-marshmallows (or you can chop larger marshmallows)
16-ounce can fruit cocktail or peaches (I prefer peaches) (drained)
1 graham-cracker pie crust

- Mix the cream cheese and marshmallows.
- Add a little juice from the fruit cocktail or peaches so the mixture doesn't get too dry (but don't make it too runny).
- Pour about half the mixture into the pie crust (just until it covers the bottom).
- Add a layer of fruit cocktail or peaches.

- Add another layer of the cream cheese–marshmallow mixture.
- Add the rest of the fruit cocktail or peaches.
- Refrigerate until you are ready to serve (at least two hours).

"Why does everyone talk about the past?
All that counts is tomorrow's game."

—Roberto Clemente

ACKNOWLEDGMENTS

I have to tell you, these acknowledgments took me the longest to write of any other page in the book. There are many people whom I owe my sincere gratitude to, not only for their help with this book, but also for their unending and unwavering support in my overall journey to rediscovery. And then there are those whom I never will be able to thank properly (e.g., the woman in the Miami airport who prompted me to get rid of my post-divorce red hair) and those whom I can never thank enough (e.g., one sister in particular who was by my side every step of the way). But I'd like to try anyway.

In no particular order, I raise a coquito to the following supporters:

Mom: I can only hope to one day be half the mother you are. I am the person I am today because of what you taught me. Despite how devastating this all has been, you stood strong and gave me hope. You took care of me and my boys like no one in this world could. Your promise of Love is our greatest gift.

Jinny: I admire your strength, your knowledge and unstoppable determination. . . . I admire YOU. You are an inspiration, always there to listen, to make me find my own answers (those were the clearest wake-up calls) and to remind me that in Life there are no problems, only opportunities. I'm so blessed to have you in my Life. . . . Thank you for your advice, for the laughter and for filling my Life with Colors.

Dad: I know that you have had to suffered as much as I did throughout all of this, and you never broke down for me. You always listen. With just my first few words on the phone, you knew exactly how I was feeling. Thanks for bringing me peace and laughter, the two things I needed the most.

Jose: The best brother-in-law Jinny could ever give me! You bring us so much happiness. I have never met anyone so willing to share their peace, wisdom, and light. You always show us ways to see the beauty in our own lives. Thank you for stepping up to the plate and being such a wonderful father figure to my boys. For reminding us that "When things don't go our way, BE THANKFUL, because there is a greater plan for us. . . ."

Jowie y Ricky: I don't know what I would do without you. Thanks for being the best brothers a little sister could ever hope for. For never losing your calm and making me laugh (many times at myself) so hard and work on my abs.

To My Family: For making every day with us so incredibly special. Abuela Aida, thank you for praying the rosary every day for our family "*y que todo me salga bien.*"

To My Colombian Family: For being there for me and my kids, for trying to cheer me up until it worked! For loving me and my boys as yours.

Tiana Rios: For all the help, for always listening, for keeping me whole. For absolutely Loving my boys. Thanks for keeping me on my toes, especially when I'm about to give in to the boys! I can't imagine Life without you.

Jennifer Nieman: The smartest businesswoman I know. For believing in me more than myself. For looking always to the future with hope and for loving me and my boys with passion. Your determination and commitment to your work are invincible. I'm the luckiest to have you on my team because I had never seen anyone who loves what they do as much as you do. And yes, answering the work phone while you are having a contraction . . . is crazy!

Melissa y Haydee: For keeping on telling me Life is Fair.

My Love: Because you make me want to be a better person. Because nothing makes you happier than to see me succeed. Most of all, for showing me that life has just began. Thank you for sharing with my boys the most pure and genuine love. . . . We absolutely love you.

Thanks To All of My Friends: To all of you who have somehow touched my life: Andy Abbad, Gladys Algarin, Noraidy Algarin, Shannon Algieri, Greg Anderson, Yesenia Bassali, Gisselle Blondet, Estella Cabrera, Gladys Calvert, Jim Calvert, Tiara Cantlin, Olga Carney, Daisy Collado, Omar Cruz, Elsa Delgado, George Leon, Isabel Lepejian, Mary Wilson, Gloria Hincapie, Eddie Olmos, Lymari Olmos, Suzanne Baptiste, Tracy Pollack, Eva Martinez, Larry Monge, Ednita Nazario, Cindy Nogue, Rosa Normandia, Lu Parker, Rose Rios, Heather Russell, Maital Sabban, Yolanda Santamaria, Cristina Saralegui, Alex Wescourt.

Eduardo Xol: Who came into my life at the perfect time. If not for our talks, this project would have been just a wish on my list. Thanks for your friendship and for introducing me to great and wonderful friends . . . like:

Raymond: Thanks for believing in this project and for your patience.

Marissa Matteo: I want to be you when I grow up! Thanks for listening and understanding my ideas. I cherish all our talks and enjoy every laughter. Remember, this is just the beginning!

My Ex-Husband: Because together we discovered so many wonderful things and apart I rediscovered myself.